Contents

Introduction

The Basic Oxford Picture Dictionary Teacher's Resource Book is an imaginative collection of low-beginning level, four-skill, communicative ESL activities to be used in conjunction with *The Basic Oxford Picture Dictionary* and *The Basic Oxford Picture Dictionary Workbook.* The Teacher's Resource Book incorporates the visuals and vocabulary of the Dictionary while employing a variety of ESL techniques and learning approaches that are student-centered and highly interactive.

Organization

The Teacher's Resource Book includes step-by-step Teacher's Notes for each of the 11 activity types featured in the book: Focused Listening I, Focused Listening II, TPR Sequence, Information Exchange, Mixer, Interview, Board Game, Language Experience Pictures, Language Experience Projects, Life Skills Reading, and Narrative Reading.

Following the Teacher's Notes are 13 activity units The first unit (A) focuses on using the Contents, the Index, and the Dictionary in general. The next 12 units correspond in content and vocabulary to the 12 units of the Dictionary.

Alphabet and Number Cards, Answer Cards, and an index to the activities appear in the appendix of the book.

Teacher's Notes

There are 11 sets of Teacher's Notes, one for each of the 11 activity types found in the Teacher's Resource Book. These notes provide basic at-a-glance information about the activity as well as mini-lesson plans for conducting the activities. The activity type, time, and grouping strategy appear at the top of the Teacher's Notes page. The activity focus and before class preparations are highlighted as well.

The lesson plan for each activity type is organized into four stages featuring numbered steps as well as options. These stages are:

- Preview   Reviewing the Dictionary topic and target vocabulary.
- Presentation   Modeling the activity and reviewing the directions.
- Practice   Setting up the activity or task.
- Follow Up   Applying or extending the lesson.

Throughout the Teacher's Notes, the phrase *For literacy-level students* is followed by suggestions for varying an activity to suit the needs of literacy-level students.

Student Activity Sheets

There are 130 reproducible activity sheets in the Teacher's Resource Book. Each unit features a tapescript page and 10 reproducible activity sheets. The tapescript page includes all the tapescripts for the Focused Listening I and II activities in a unit. Each tapescript gives the activity type (Focused Listening I or II) and cross references the activity sheet (if there is one) in that unit. Each activity sheet indicates the corresponding activity type, Teacher's Notes, and Dictionary page(s).

Appendix

The Appendix contains four pages of reproducible materials: Alphabet Cards, Number Cards, Answer Cards (Yes/No/Not Sure), and a "Don't Look" Mask (for masking vocabulary on the dictionary page). These materials are useful for practicing letter and number recognition (crucial for Dictionary work), forming pairs and small groups, and for checking comprehension of target vocabulary or directions. The last pages of the Appendix contain an Index that cross-references activities by type and title.

Activity Types
The Basic Oxford Picture Dictionary Teacher's Resource Book contains 11 different activity types that are described below.

Focused Listening I
These activities give students a chance to hear English spoken in real-life situations, with background noise, pauses, and interruptions. In addition, students listen for specific information embedded within the natural-paced speech. While listening, they demonstrate comprehension by pointing to pictures in their dictionaries. These listening exercises can help students transfer their listening skills to the real world.

Procedure
The teacher plays the Teacher's Resource Book Cassette or reads the tapescript that contains the Dictionary vocabulary, while the students point to the appropriate pictures in the Dictionary. The listening passage allows students to practice recognizing the previously taught vocabulary in a natural listening situation.

Helpful Ideas
- Literacy-level students often have superior listening skills. Call on them to demonstrate the pointing or have them circulate to assist other students.
- Teach the vocabulary in a separate lesson **before** students hear the listening passage. (See **Using *The Basic Oxford Picture Dictionary*,** p. x.)
- Tell students (or have them predict) what the listening passage is about.
- Reassure students that they can hear the listening passage as many times as needed. Each time they listen they will hear more.
- Do not hesitate to stop the tape, rewind it, and let students listen again. Repeated listening allows students to feel successful and it reinforces their listening skills.

Focused Listening II
As in Focused Listening I activities, students listen to English spoken in real-life situations, with background noise, pauses, and interruptions. They also listen for specific information embedded within natural-paced speech. Using activity sheets, students demonstrate comprehension by completing a task, such as circling a word or checking a specific category.

Procedure
The teacher plays the cassette or reads the tapescript while students mark their activity sheets. In some cases, two different activities involve the same tapescript. In such cases, activity sheets feature a dotted fold line, allowing students to focus on one task at a time.

Helpful Ideas (See Focused Listening I, above)
- Be sure that literacy-level students can identify the choices on the activity sheet.
- Write the first example on the board (or use an overhead projector) so that students are comfortable with the task.
- Stop the tape between items so that students have time to mark their papers.

TPR Sequence

These activities are based on James Asher's Total Physical Response (TPR) theory. In the early stages of language learning, students can use non-verbal responses to verify their understanding of language they may not yet be able to produce. Also, because students are encouraged to move, even stand, during the activity, TPR Sequence provides a welcome break from sitting and using a book.

Procedure

The teacher mimes the sequence featured on the activity sheet while students act out the commands. Students then give the commands to one another, or sequence the pictures. In additional follow-up options, students can match the pictures to the words or write statements based on the pictures.

Helpful Ideas

- Have literacy-level students play "Concentration" with the cut-up commands and pictures.
- Bring in realia or props to add excitement to the sequence presentation.
- Encourage participation by over-dramatizing the actions yourself and by giving positive feedback to those students who are participating.
- Do TPR activities with any vocabulary in the Dictionary by having students point to the pictures as you describe them. Also, ask students to manipulate classroom objects in response to commands and to follow simple exercise commands at least once or twice a week.

Information Exchange

These activities give students practice in real communication. Students work in pairs to exchange information that is missing from their activity sheets. In some info exchange activities, such as **Domingo's Retiring!** (p. 54), students have identical pictures with different items missing. In others, such as **Describe Me** (p. 42), each student has both a picture and a checklist. Information Exchanges contain a degree of unpredictability as students ask and answer each other's questions.

Procedure

Student pairs use an open manila folder as a screen between them. One student has the "A" activity sheet, the other has the "B" activity sheet. "A" asks questions of "B" to complete the missing items. "B" then asks questions of "A". When they have completed the task, students compare activity sheets.

Helpful Ideas

- Allow literacy-level students to look at each other's pages after each question.
- Be sure to model the activity adequately so that students are prepared to do it on their own.
- To help students communicate in English, pair stronger students and weaker students or students from different language groups.
- To create a more realistic conversational atmosphere, have partners sit facing each other.

Mixer

These activities give students a chance to walk around the room meeting their classmates. Mixers also give students practice in asking and answering questions using a simple format. In some mixers, such as **Who Lives in Your House?** (p. 56), the questions require a simple "Yes" or "No" answer. In others, such as **What Size Do You Wear?** (p. 104), students respond with short answers.

Procedure
All students get the same activity sheet and fill in the missing letters or words. Then the teacher practices the questions with the whole class. Next, students walk around the room finding the students whose responses fit the blanks on their activity sheet. When all the blanks have been filled in, or after a specified time limit, students return to their seats to share their answers with the whole class.

Helpful Ideas
- If you have space in your classroom, ask students to come to the front or back of the room to "mix." In this way students are more likely to talk with a greater number of people. Consider using a hallway if your room is very small.

Interview
Working in pairs, students interview each other to fill in their activity sheet. Although the questions are already written, students must listen carefully to the answers in order to complete the task on the bottom of the sheet. Interviews are structured to give students practice with beginning level grammar.

Procedure
Both students receive the same activity sheet. First they read the questions silently and write their answers in the "My Answers" column. Then they ask their partner the same questions in order to fill out the "My Partner's Answers" column. Students are then able to complete the statements below the questionnaire .

Helpful Ideas
- Pair literacy-level students with helpful, tactful partners who will model how to write answers or spell for them.
- To pair students randomly, duplicate a class set of the activity sheet in two different colors. Distribute a different color to each side of your class. Ask students to find a partner with a different color activity sheet.

Board Game
Played in small groups, board games give additional reading and speaking practice with previously learned vocabulary. Because the directions cover all four basic skills, a lot of variety is possible in this simple activity.

Procedure
Each small group gets one activity sheet. Students take turns flipping a coin and moving around the board following the directions on the spaces.

Helpful Ideas
- Since all the board games share the same directions, take plenty of time to explain and model the directions the first time through. Later, when students play the game again with a different topic, you won't need to concentrate as much on the directions.

Language Experience Approach (LEA) Picture

These activities provide reading and writing practice even for very beginning students. Because students create a story themselves, they are reading words with which they are already familiar. An important part of LEA is for the teacher to write the story exactly as the students tell it. By doing so, the teacher ensures that students read their own words and have an opportunity to predict and self-correct their language.

Procedure

All students receive the same activity sheet. The teacher elicits a story from the students about the picture and writes that story on the board. After helping the teacher edit the story on the board, students copy it onto their activity sheets. They then practice reading the story to one another.

Helpful Ideas

- Be sure to call on literacy-level students to help tell the story. Have them practice reading the passage several times with a partner. In the follow-up, call on them to erase the words from the board, with directions, such as "Erase a word that begins with B."
- Ask a lot of questions about the picture before writing the story so that students are comfortable with using the vocabulary needed.

Language Experience Approach (LEA) Project

These activities are more active versions of LEA Picture activities. Students first do a class project, such as designing a classroom or making sandwiches following written directions. When they finish, they dictate a story to the teacher about what they did.

Procedure

Students use the activity sheet to guide them through the class project (usually 30 minutes or more). When the project is completed, the teacher elicits from the students a story about how the project was done or its result. Students help the teacher edit the story on the board, then copy it into their notebooks. Finally, the students practice reading the story to one another.

Helpful Ideas

- Assemble in advance all the materials needed for the project, such as markers or glue. When possible, have students bring some of the supplies themselves. For example, for **Sandwich Shop** (p. 82) students can bring in some of the sandwich ingredients.

Life Skills Reading

These activities give students practice in reading practical information, such as forms, signs, and want ads, which feature vocabulary from the unit. Each activity includes a written section as a comprehension check.

Procedure

Each student receives an activity sheet. The teacher presents the reading materials and models the first exercise, then students work on their own to complete the activity sheet.

Helpful Ideas

- Bring in realia or items similar to those depicted on the activity sheet; for example, an actual telephone bill for **A Phone Bill** (p. 35) or old prescription bottles for **Prescription Labels** (p. 119).
- Have literacy-level students focus on adding to and identifying the realia.

Narrative Reading

These activities give students practice in reading stories. As in Life Skills Reading, students demonstrate comprehension by answering questions or completing statements at the bottom of the activity sheet.

Procedure

Each student receives an activity sheet and reads the story silently. The teacher models the exercise that follows the story. Then students work on their own to complete the activity sheet.

Helpful Ideas

- Have literacy-level students listen and follow as you or an advanced student read the passage and questions. Then talk about them.
- Discuss the picture thoroughly before students read the story. Ask absurd questions using familiar words, such as "Is the little boy her husband?" or "Is the woman a mother or a father?" This gives stronger students a chance to demonstrate their knowledge and weaker students a chance to review the vocabulary.

Using *The Basic Oxford Picture Dictionary*

The Basic Oxford Picture Dictionary is first and foremost a dictionary. Before students can effectively use the Dictionary, they need to be able to identify the alphabet and the numbers 1–100. Once students can quickly identify and use the letters and numbers, they need to learn how to use the Dictionary's Contents and Index. The activities in unit A of the Teacher's Resource Book will help familiarize students with these important elements of the Dictionary.

Using the Alphabet Cards and Number Cards

The alphabet and number cards in the Appendix are excellent tools for acquainting students with the letters and numbers in the Dictionary, and helping students find words using the alphabetical arrangement of the Index.

- Begin by duplicating and distributing a class set of each of the alphabet and number sheets. Have students first use the sheets without cutting the letters or numbers apart. Have students listen and point to the letters or numbers as you read them in order and then at random.
- Cut apart one set of alphabet or number cards and distribute one card each to 26 students (28, if numbered cards are used). Ask the students with the cards to come to the front of the room and line up in the correct order. Once these students are in a line, ask the seated students to verify the order using their sheets.
- Have students cut their sheets of letters or numbers apart to create their own sets of cards. (Cards may be clipped together, placed in small envelopes, or kept in pocket folders for easy storage.) Have students scramble their cards and rearrange them in order.
- Once students are familiar with the alphabet and numbers, call out a letter or a number and have students pick up that card and the cards that come before and after it.
- Spell a word from the Dictionary (with no double letters) and have students spell it out using their own sets of alphabet cards. Once students have the word, have them write it in their notebooks. When students have a list of four or five words, introduce the skill of alphabetizing and have students find the words in the Index.
- Select a page in the Dictionary and have students take turns pulling one of the number cards out of a box (1–20) and finding the vocabulary item on the Dictionary page.

Selecting Dictionary Topics

The 12 topics in the Dictionary—Everyday Language People, Family, The Home, The Market, Meal Time, Clothes, Health, Transportation, The Community, Work, and Recreation—may be approached in any order. In fact, much of the vocabulary featured in the first unit, Everyday Language, can be spread out over a course and taught in conjunction with other topics. Likewise, the grammatical structures underpinning the Teacher's Resource Book activities (in the directions and examples) can be used throughout the semester.

• Do a low-level needs assessment using the Contents pages of the Dictionary. Use the icons next to each topic to help students choose three topics they want to know more about. Take a vote and see where students' interests lie. If students' interests conflict with your course syllabus, try to include at least one Dictionary page for the most popular topic as additional practice for the class.

Presenting Vocabulary

Students need to experience the target vocabulary in more than one context. Use the stategies that follow to contextualize the vocabulary and give students multiple opportunities to hear and say the words.

• Present a situation in which the target vocabulary would be used. Use realia, visuals, or mime to help students comprehend the situation. Distribute a class set of "Don't Look" Masks from the Appendix and have students cover the words at the bottom of the Dictionary page. Review the vocabulary in the context of the art on the Dictionary page and have students point to the target vocabulary and other items on the page. Have students remove the mask and look at the words.

• Direct students to look at a particular item on the Dictionary page. Use early production questioning (a sequence of questions that require student to use non-verbal or single word responses) to help students acquire the word.

(Non-verbal response)	Point to the number 1.
(Yes/No question)	Is it a pencil?
(Or question)	Is it a pencil or a pen?
(Leading statement)	I'm holding one now.
	It's a _____.
(Wh-question)	What's this?

• Check students' comprehension of the vocabulary by having them mask the words at the bottom of the page. Distribute a class set of the Yes/No Answer Cards only, and ask Yes/No questions about the vocabulary. "Is number five an eraser?" "Do I use this to write?" "Is number six wearing shoes?" Students silently hold up their cards in response to the questions, making it easy to see at a glance which students need more exposure to the vocabulary.

Working with Literacy-Level Students

If you have a mixed-level class (and who doesn't?), the beginning readers in your class will have special needs. Suggestions for accommodating those needs can be found in the Teacher's Notes, highlighted by the phrase *For your literacy-level students,* as well as in the **Activity Types** section of this Introduction (p. vi). The following suggestions will help teachers working with beginning readers in multi-level settings.

- Create a supportive atmosphere, an important factor in any classroom, by encouraging students to learn each other's names and something about each other's general interests. This supportive atmosphere is essential to literacy-level students because it helps them to feel more comfortable giving and receiving assistance from one another. Peer assistance is crucial for effective teaching because the teacher cannot check every student's work.
- Help students think of their work as "unfinished" rather than "wrong."
- Draw on the special skills most literacy-level adults have developed, such as quickness in listening, auditory memories, prediction skills, and acting skills.
- Encourage the more advanced students in your class to be peer tutors, explain that by teaching we often reinforce our own understanding.

Dictation is an important technique for the literacy-level lesson. It combines listening, spelling, writing, and clarification skills. Students will benefit by being able to spell (or request the spelling of) any word they cannot pronounce, hear, understand, or read.

- Each day ask a different student to lead a brief warm-up activity by having them dictate words or phrases from previous lessons.
- During a dictation, encourage students to refer to their Dictionaries to check their work or request spellings.
- Follow up the dictation by asking volunteers to write the dictated words on the board. Have seated students use their Dictionaries to check the responses on the board and their own work against the words in the Dictionaries.
- Have students, in pairs, take turns dictating five words randomly chosen from a specific Dictionary page. One student looks at the Dictionary and dictates the words, the other writes them on a sheet of paper. After each one has had a turn, the partners look in their Dictionaries to find the words they've written. (Low- to high-beginning students benefit from this type of activity as well.)

Classroom Management Tips

Highly interactive activities in a low-level ESL classroom require a few special management techniques to be successful.

First, all necessary materials need to be assembled before class. (While you will want to be sure all the materials are available, it's a real time-saver to have students cut, distribute, or organize materials in the opening period of the class.) Next, check for understanding at each step of the lesson to make sure that students are ready to continue with the activity. It's also necessary to allow sufficient time for the Practice stage and to monitor student participation during the Practice. Finally, to keep interaction in the target language and student interest level high, it's vital to pair students with a variety of partners.

Assembling Materials

The Materials section of the Teacher's Notes specifies the materials, Dictionary page(s), and activity sheet required for a particular activity. Be sure to check this section ahead of time. The "Before class" section of the Teacher's Notes indicates the duplicating and cutting needs of an activity. If cut lines appear on an activity sheet, consider having students do the cutting as a TPR activity.

To store the cut-up, reproducible pictures, sentences, Answer Cards, "Don't Look" Mask, Alphabet Cards, and Number Cards, use class sets of envelopes or have students create their own storage pockets by stapling half-sheets of construction paper to both sides of manila folders. These pocket folders of manipulatives can then be taken home for practice or filed alphabetically in a file box in the classroom.

Facilitating the Activity

Checking comprehension is crucial before beginning any activity. To see if students understand the language to be used in an activity, as well as the activity's directions, use the Answer Cards. Students can rarely answer the question "Do you understand?" honestly without losing face. However, with a Yes/No question about the topic, target vocabulary, or directions for an activity, students can easily respond non-verbally by holding up their Yes/No/Not Sure cards. This technique provides you with a very clear picture of the varying levels of student comprehension in the classroom.

- After presenting the directions for an activity, try these questions: "Do you work alone?" "Can you write short answers?" "How many names do you need?" Also, try using "or" questions: "Do you write or say the answers?" By providing students with an answer, you'll get a more effective choral response.

    Monitoring, or being aware of what's going on during an activity, is the teacher's most important role during the Practice stage. This is the best time to assess how the activity is going and if it is meeting your students' needs.

- To monitor listening activities when using a cassette, stay close to the tape player while it's playing, but move around the room when you pause between items or check students' responses at the end of an exercise. You might also ask your more advanced students to help you monitor their classmates' progress on repeat listenings.

- While students work in pairs or small groups, circulate to observe their progress and to answer any questions. Try not to interrupt them with numerous corrections. Instead, make a mental note of problem areas for future instruction.

    Heterogeneous grouping is an important factor in interactive activities. To eliminate first language interference, have students work in mixed-language groups. Of course, if this is not always possible, have students form mixed-ability or mixed-gender groups.

- To pair students, distribute upper-case Alphabet Cards to half the class and matching lower-case Alphabet Cards to the other half. (The distribution of cards can be manipulated so that upper-case letter holders are higher-level students, one language group, or one gender.) Direct students to find their partner by walking around the classroom asking classmates, "Do you have _____?" Once pairs are formed, have partners sit together and continue with the first stage of the activity. Students can also use the number cards 1–9 to match up by same number, two numbers that total 10, or odds and evens.

- To form heterogeneous groups, take some time to mentally identify the homogeneous groups in your class (language groups, ages, level). Distribute one kind of card to each group. (All Spanish speakers get #1 or A, all Armenian speakers get #2 or B, and so on.) Direct students to form groups of four different numbers or letters.

    Time limits and quiet signals are effective ways to manage the silence and the noise of interactive activities. Students need to know the parameters of a communicative task, including the time it takes to complete the task. Once time has been called, students need to focus on the follow-up. The use of a quiet signal allows students to shift gears between the stages of an activity.

- Vary your quiet signals so that they retain their punch. A few effective signals are flicking the lights on and off, ringing a bell, raising your hand and—as one creative teacher we know does—playing a harmonica!

Audio-Visual Equipment

Tape Players

A tape player brings to life any focused listening exercise. While the tapescript in the Teacher's Resource Book may be read aloud, using a tape player allows for repeated listenings with the same tempo and same intonation. A tape player with a pause button enables you to easily stop the tape between items or pause to highlight a particular section of the listening passage.

Each activity on the cassette references the unit and activity page number in the Teacher's Resource Book. However, a tape player with a counter will enable you to quickly note the location of specific passages on the cassette. (Remember to insert the cassette, rewind, and reset the counter to 000 before you fast forward to the desired numbers.)

Spend a little time practicing with the rewind button too, because it's not unusual to have to repeat an item up to five times. A light touch on the button will usually replay the last item heard.

Overhead Projectors (OHPs)

Teachers fortunate enough to have an OHP in their classroom will find using transparencies of the activity sheets very helpful. The entire class can focus on all or a just portion of the sheet while you set up the activity. You or volunteers can write directly on the transparency to model the activity or to verify correct responses after the activity. In the case of TPR Sequence activities, revealing one picture at a time is an effective way of building suspense and keeping students focused on the activity.

You may also want to use the Overhead Transparencies available for *The Basic Oxford Picture Dictionary.* By selectively masking sections of the pictures on the transparency, you can focus on a particular part of a Dictionary page. This technique is especially useful when you want to verify student comprehension of a particular vocabulary item, or ask questions about one portion of a specific scene.

Teacher's Notes
for Units A-12

Focused Listening I

Focus: Students listen to recorded monologues and conversations, and point to specific items or people in the Dictionary as they are mentioned.

Materials: Dictionaries; listening cassette; selected tapescript; "Don't Look" Masks, p. 171; Answer Cards, p. 171

Before class, look over the tapescript, taking note of the boldfaced target vocabulary. In addition, look over the dictionary pages indicated on the tapescript.

Preview Options

■ Distribute the Answer Cards. Have students open their dictionaries to the page specified on the tapescript. Ask Yes/No questions about the people, items, or situations depicted on the dictionary page. Have students hold up the Answer Cards in response to your questions.

■ Write the activity title on the board and have students open their dictionaries to the page specified on the tapescript. Have the class predict the content of the tape based on the activity title and the pictures on the dictionary page.

Presentation

1. Tell students that they will be listening to the tape and pointing to pictures in their dictionaries.

2. Have students open their dictionaries to the page indicated on the tapescript. Distribute the masks and have students cover the vocabulary at the bottom of the page. Assure students that they will have several opportunities to hear the listening passage.

3. Play the tape through the first segment of the tapescript. (The end of each segment is marked by an asterisk.) Stop the tape and check to be sure that students are pointing to the correct picture. Replay this section of the tape until all students are pointing to the same picture.

Practice

4. Play the tape, stopping after each segment when necessary. Replay the tape or individual segments two to five times.

5. Play the tape one last time and pause after each segment. Have volunteers call out the number of the dictionary item or person referred to on the tape. Get class consensus on the accuracy of the responses.

Follow-Up Options

■ Create a "new word" list with the class, identifying those words in the tapescript that students would like to learn. Whenever possible, use pictures from the dictionary or other sources to help define the new words.

■ Make a list of expressions such as "Uh," "Hmmm," "Huh?" or "Yeah?" and categorize them as expressions that give speakers time to think, check their understanding, or show their interest.

For literacy level students, unmask the vocabulary at the bottom of the page. Play the tape again and have students point to the target words they hear.

Focused Listening II

Focus: Students listen to recorded conversations for specific information. While students are listening, they circle, check off, number, or categorize the correct information.

Materials: Dictionaries; a class set of the selected Focused Listening II activity sheet; selected tapescript; listening cassette; "Don't Look" Masks, p. 171; and Answer Cards, p. 171

Before class, look over the tapescript, activity sheet, and dictionary page(s) indicated on the activity sheet. Duplicate a class set of the activity sheet, and copy the example onto the board.

Preview Options

Ask Wh-questions related to the activity sheet's content, such as "What are some foods you order at a restaurant?" or "Who are some workers you see every day?" List the answers on the board. Include target vocabulary from the tapescript.

Have students open their dictionaries to one of the pages specified on the activity sheet and mask the vocabulary at the bottom of that page. Ask students to study the page for 60 seconds, close their books, and work with a partner to orally list who or what they saw. Repeat this activity with other pages specified on the tapescript.

Presentation

. Tell students that they will be listening for the information necessary to complete their activity sheets. Help students predict the content of the listening passage by discussing the title, text, and pictures on the activity sheet.

. Use the example on the board to explain the task to the students. Assure them that they will have several opportunities to hear the listening passage.

. Have students listen to the tape through the first item on the tapescript, then review the example on the board.

. Distribute the activity sheet. (If there is a second exercise on the activity sheet, have students fold their papers as indicated.) Go over the directions with the class and check students' comprehension by asking Yes/No questions, such as "Do you circle the information?" or "Do you make a check?" Have students respond non-verbally to your questions by raising their answer cards.

For literacy level students, before moving on to the practice stage, go over all the numbers, words, or pictures on the activity sheet. As first you, then volunteers, say a number or word or describe a picture, have students point to it on the activity sheet.

Practice

5. Play the tape, stopping after each item if necessary.

6. Survey student responses to each item. Get class consensus on the accuracy of the responses. Replay the items two to five times until all responses are accurate.

7. Where there is a second exercise on the activity sheet, explain the new listening focus and follow steps 1–6 above.

Follow-Up Options

■ Ask volunteers to give information that parallels the content of the tapescript. For example, ask students to say what time they wake up. Then ask the class to recall what was said.

■ Have students form questions using the vocabulary from the activity sheet. For example, **get up:** "What time do you get up?"

■ Have students restate in their own words what they heard on the tape.

TPR Sequence

Focus: Students use a series of picture cues to respond to commands and act out an action sequence.

Materials: Dictionaries; two class sets of the selected TPR Sequence activity sheet; appropriate realia and/or pictures; scissors

Before class, look over the commands on the activity sheet and gather the realia and/or pictures. Duplicate two class sets of the activity sheet, keeping the sets separate.

Preview

1. Have students open their dictionaries to one of the pages specified on the activity sheet. Hold up the realia or demonstrate the actions from the activity sheet and ask students to use their dictionaries to identify the item or action.

For literacy level students, choose four to six words from the selected TPR sequence that students can already read. Help the class create commands or sentences using these words as you write them on the board.

Presentation

2. Demonstrate the actions from the TPR sequence, making statements in the simple present. For example, in **Sit Down and Study,** p. 29, you would make the statement "First, I sit at my desk." while sitting down at your desk. Repeat this step once or twice, asking questions about what you're doing. For example,"I'm sitting at my desk. Am I sitting or standing?"

3. Ask three to five volunteers to come to the front of the room. Give the TPR commands and demonstrate the actions with the volunteers. Ask the other students in the class questions, such as "Are the notebooks open?" "Are we sitting or standing?" One word responses are acceptable.

4. Give the TPR commands and have the whole class perform the actions with you. Then give the commands without modeling and observe students' accuracy.

5. Have the class respond as you give the TPR commands out of sequence. Throw in a novel or absurd command, such as "Pick up your desk." that incorporates language from the original sequence and previously introduced words. Then ask volunteers to give you commands from the sequence. Make a few mistakes in order to force the class to correct you.

6. Distribute the first set of activity sheets and scissors to the class and have students cut apart the pictures and the sentences. Have students put aside the sentence strips and lay the pictures out face up. Call out the commands and have students hold up the appropriate pictures.

For literacy level students, copy the sentences from the activity sheet onto the board. Have the students read the sentences and perform the actions.

Practice Options

■ To practice oral production, pair students and designate one "teacher" and one "student" in each pair. Have the teachers put the pictures face down in front of them, and pick one, concealing it from their students. Teachers then use the picture cues to give commands to their students. Have pairs switch roles and repeat the activity.

■ To practice sequencing, divide the class into groups of four. Distribute scrambled sets of sentences to each group. Have the students take turns choosing two sentences each, read their cues, and work together to put them in order.

Follow-Up Options

■ Distribute the second set of activity sheets. Have students match the written commands to the pictures.

■ Have students write a statement for each picture, using the commands as clues. For example: "He's sitting at his desk."

For literacy level students, have student pairs play "Concentration" with the cut-up pictures and written commands from the activity sheet. Have students match the commands to the appropriate pictures.

Information Exchange

Focus: Paired students elicit information from each other to complete different activity sheets.

Materials: Dictionaries; half a class set each of the selected Information Exchange activity sheets A and B; manila folders (one per pair). Optional: "Don't Look" Masks, paper bag, and appropriate realia.

Before class, look over the A and B activity sheets, taking note of the sample question(s), example(s), and target vocabulary. Duplicate half a class set of each sheet, keeping the sets separate.

Preview Options

Have students open their dictionaries to the page specified on the activity sheet and mask the vocabulary at the bottom of the page. Call out the target vocabulary and ask students to point to the appropriate pictures in their dictionaries.

Use the paper bag to hide an item or picture related to the selected dictionary topic. Announce the topic to the class and ask students to guess what's in the bag.

For literacy level students, have students open their dictionaries to the page specified on the activity sheet. Call out the target vocabulary and ask students to point to the pictures first and then the words at the bottom of the page.

Presentation

. Tell students that they will take turns asking for and giving missing information in order to fill in their activity sheets.

. On the board, write a sample statement or question that students will need to do the activity. Model the sentence, substituting vocabulary students will use. Discuss different clarification strategies, such as, "Say that again, please."

. Have students practice making new sentences or questions using the clarification strategies presented in Step 2.

4. Pair students and assign each one an A or a B role. Explain that students will each have a paper with different information.

5. Distribute a manila folder to each pair, to be propped up between the students as a screen.

6. Distribute the A and B activity sheets to the appropriate partners. Review the directions. Check for comprehension by asking A students a question that only they will able to answer. Do the same for B students.

7. Have one student pair demonstrate the activity, using the manila folder as a screen.

For literacy level students, distribute only the A activity sheets to all students. Call out target vocabulary and have students point to the words. Dictate the information students will need to complete the activity sheet. After each item, write the answer on the board. Distribute the B sheets to the class and follow the same procedure.

Practice

8. Have students, in pairs, ask and answer questions to complete their activity sheets.

9. Walk around the room and monitor student progress. Help with clarification questions as necessary.

Follow-Up

10. Have students check their answers by comparing activity sheets.

Mixer

Focus: Students circulate, randomly asking and answering questions using their activity sheets as cues.

Materials: Dictionaries; a class set of the selected Mixer activity sheet; Answer Cards, p. 171, "Don't Look" Masks, p. 171

Before class, look over the question(s) on the activity sheet, taking note of the target vocabulary. Duplicate a class set of the activity sheet.

Preview

- Distribute the Answer Cards. Ask Yes/No questions relating to the activity sheet. For example, in **Who Lives in Your House?** p. 56, ask, "Do you live with your sister?" "Do you live with your mother?" Have students hold up the Answer Cards in response to your questions.

- Have students open their dictionaries to the page(s) specified on the activity sheet and mask the vocabulary at the bottom of the page. Have students name the items or the actions depicted.

  For literacy level students, have each person dictate his or her name to the class while the other students write it down.

Presentation

1. Tell students that they will be walking around the classroom talking to their classmates in order to fill in their activity sheets.

2. Using the board, model the questions that students will need for the activity, and the various responses. Discuss different clarification strategies, such as "Please repeat that."

3. Have students practice asking and answering the questions with the person next to them.

4. Distribute the activity sheet. If the activity sheet requires students to write in missing letters or words, model the example on the board.

5. Direct students, working alone or in pairs, to fill in the missing items. Write an example of the completed activity sheet on the board. Have students correct their papers.

   For literacy level students, read each question and have students point to the question or cue on the activity sheet. Have students use their dictionaries if necessary.

6. Invite two volunteers to the front of the room. Have one volunteer ask the other the first question. The volunteer completes the item by asking, "How do you spell your name?" and writes the other student's name in the appropriate box. When appropriate, point out that students should try to fill both the "yes" and "no" boxes to each question.

   For literacy level students, have students read the questions using the cues.

Practice

7. Have students circulate to complete their activity sheets. Monitor student practice by walking around and checking papers.

Follow-Up

8. After the mixer is completed, have students share their various answers with the class. Discuss the results with the class.

Interview

Focus: Students work in pairs asking and answering questions that relate dictionary topics to their personal lives.

Materials: Dictionaries; a class set of the selected Interview activity sheet

Before class, look over the activity sheet, taking note of the questions and grammar structure. Duplicate a class set of the activity sheet, and copy the grid and questions from the interview portion onto the board.

Preview Options

Create heterogeneous pairs. Have students practice the interview process by taking turns asking for and giving their names and birthplaces.

Copy an affirmative and negative statement from the second half of the activity sheet, such as "I exercise." "I don't exercise." Explain the grammar that supports the statements and have the students take turns making the statements about themselves, you, and their classmates.

For literacy level students, have students pair, introduce themselves, and practice spelling their names to each other.

Presentation

. Write the title of the selected interview on the board. Tell students that they will be interviewing their partners on this topic and reporting on the information they learn.

. Have the class practice asking each of the questions written on the board.

. Using the grid on the board, explain that students fill out the "My Answers" section of the grid first, by themselves, and then ask their partners the questions.

. Demonstrate the procedure with a volunteer. Have the volunteer fill in the grid with his or her answers, then ask you the questions and fill out the grid with your answers. Point out that when a yes/no answer is not appropriate, a one-word response is fine.

Practice

5. Distribute the Interview section of the activity sheet to each student. Have students do the first section of the grid on their own, within a time limit of two to three minutes.

   For literacy level students, distribute the activity sheet and have students find the questions as you read them. Repeat the questions several times, then ask students to circle key words as you call them out.

6. Set a 10-minute time limit for students to interview their partners. Circulate and monitor student practice.

7. Call time and have students complete the second half of the sheet, circling the correct information. Have partners check each other's papers.

Follow-Up Options

■ Have pairs form (or recreate) a group of four. Have students in the group report on their partners. Students can use the activity sheet to assist them in making their reports, but they should not be reading from the sheet.

■ Use the responses from each pair to chart the entire class' preferences. Create a bar graph or a pie chart to show which items got the strongest response from the class as a whole. Ask students to look at the graph and make general statements about the class.

Board Game

Focus: Students practice answering a variety of questions based on a particular dictionary topic.

Materials: Dictionaries; one copy of a selected Board Game activity sheet for every four students; coins; scratch paper; 12 index cards, and scissors

Before class, look over the activity sheet, taking note of each space on the game board. Duplicate a quarter class set of the activity sheet and copy it onto the board, filling in only the first three squares. (For literacy level classes, you'll need a full class set of the activity sheet.) For the Follow-Up Option, write a different command and/or question (related to the activity sheet topic) on each of the 12 index cards. Write the numbers 1–12 on the backs of the cards.

Preview Options

■ Have students open their dictionaries to the page(s) specified on the activity sheet. Ask students a few questions from the board game activity sheet and have students find the answers on the dictionary page.

■ Ask students to tell you what games they've played in their countries. Preview the following vocabulary during the discussion: rules, taking turns, game board, marker, and flip.

Presentation

1. Tell students that they are going to play a game to improve their vocabulary and give them practice asking and answering questions.

2. Demonstrate how to play the game using the copy of the game on the board. Ask three volunteers to write their names on separate pieces of scratch paper, while you do the same. Tape these papers to the "Start" space on the board. Explain that the papers are the markers for the game and that each player must respond to the command on the "Start" space.

3. Show the class a coin and demonstrate flipping it "heads" and "tails." Flip the coin and move your marker to the correct space: one space for heads, two spaces for tails. Read the directions or question in the space aloud. Make your response and get class consensus on its accuracy.

4. Give each volunteer two turns in front of the class.

For literacy level students, distribute a class set of activity sheets before beginning the Practice section of the activity. Read the spaces on the game board out of order and have students point to the correct space on their activity sheets.

Practice Options

■ Divide the class into groups of four and distribute an activity sheet to each group. Give students a time limit (15 to 20 minutes) and circulate while the groups play the game.

■ Identify one advanced student to sit with each group of four (forming a group of five.) Have the advanced student referee the game.

■ Pair students and have two pairs play each other. Partners must agree on the answers they give.

Follow-Up Option

■ Divide the class into two teams, A and B. Using the activity sheet already on the board, substitute numbers for the directions on the spaces. Have team members take turns flipping coins. As a team lands on a space, a team representative responds to the question or command on the corresponding index card.

LEA Picture

Focus: Students work together to dictate a story about a picture and read the story they've created.

Materials: Dictionaries; a class set of the selected Language Experience activity sheet; "Don't Look" Masks, p. 171

Before class, look over the activity sheet, taking note of the target vocabulary depicted. Duplicate a class set of the activity sheet.

Preview

. Have students open their dictionaries to the page(s) specified on the activity sheet and mask the vocabulary at the bottom of the page. Have students tell you the items or people they see on the page.

For literacy level students, don't use the "Masks." Have students use the vocabulary at the bottom of the page as a reference.

Presentation

. Tell students that they will be looking at a picture and working as a class to write a story about the picture.

. Distribute the activity sheets and discuss the title, the people in the picture, and the situation depicted.

. Ask questions to elicit more specific information about the picture. Sequence your questions so that you use several Yes/No, then Either/Or, then Leading Statements and, finally, Wh-questions. For **The Burglary,** p. 46, sample questions would be "Is the driver a man?" "Is the woman young or old?" "The man is carrying a ____" "What is he taking from the apartment?"

Practice

5. Remind students that they don't need their pencils for this part of the practice, because they will be **talking** while you are writing.

6. Using general and specific questions, elicit from students a story about, or a description of, the picture they've just discussed. For **The Burglary,** p. 46, a sample general question would be "What's happening in the apartment?" A specific question would be "What is the man carrying?" Write the story on the board exactly as the students tell it to you. (Be careful not to use Yes/No questions at this stage.)

7. Read the story aloud once, pausing at places where the grammatical structure is incorrect. Give students an opportunity to edit their work by asking questions, such as "Is there another way to say this? Is this okay?" If the entire class approves an incorrect grammar structure, **do not** correct the error at this time. Address the error in a follow-up lesson.

8. Read the story aloud with the class several times.

Follow-Up Options

■ Have students copy the story onto their activity sheets and take turns reading the story to a partner.

■ Have students circle specific letters or consonant clusters on their activity sheet according to your directions. For example, "Circle the words that start with 'st.'"

■ Have students copy the story onto their activity sheets. Erase key words from the story on the board. Ask students to find these missing words in their own copies of the story. Have volunteers come to the board and write the missing words while the other students circle the words at their desks.

■ For more advanced students, make several copies of the story cut the sentences apart and scramble them. Have students sequence the sentences and check the sequence against their own copies of the story.

LEA Project

Focus: Students work together to complete a class project, dictate a story about the experience, and read the story they've created.

Materials: Dictionaries; a class set of a selected Language Experience Project activity sheet; a class set of all materials underlined on the activity sheet; "Don't Look" Masks, p. 171

Before class, look over the directions on the activity sheet, and gather the necessary materials. Duplicate a class set of the acitvity sheet.

Preview

1. Have students open their dictionaries to the page(s) specified on the activity sheet and mask the vocabulary at the bottom of the page. Have students tell you the items or people they see on the page.

   For literacy level students, don't mask the vocabulary at the bottom of the dictionary page. Let students use the vocabulary as a reference.

Presentation

2. Tell students that they will be working together on a class project and writing a story about the completed project.

3. Preview the directions on the activity sheet by demonstrating the project to the class.

4. Distribute the activity sheets and read the directions aloud with the class. Check comprehension by asking Yes/No questions, such as "Do you write or draw?" "Do you work alone or with a partner?"

5. Have students begin working on the project. Monitor students' progress by circulating and asking questions to elicit the language that students will be using when they describe their project.

Practice

6. Remind students that they don't need their pencils for this part of the practice, because they will be **talking** while you are writing.

7. Ask students a series of questions to elicit a description of the project they've just completed, such as "What did we make?" "What did we do first?" or "How did you feel while your were working?". Write the description on the board exactly as the students tell it to you.

8. Read the description aloud once, pausing at places where the grammatical structure is incorrect. Give students an opportunity to edit their work by asking questions, such as "Is there another way to say this? Is this okay?" If the class approves an incorrect grammar structure, **do not** correct the error at this time. Address the error in a follow-up lesson.

9. Read the description aloud with the class several times.

Follow-Up Options

■ Have students copy the description in their notebooks and take turns reading it to a partner.

■ Have students circle specific letters or consonant clusters in the description according to your directions. For example, "Circle the words that start with 'st'."

■ Have students copy the description into their notebooks. Erase key words from the description on the board. Have volunteers come to the board and write the missing words while the other students circle the words in their notebooks at their desks.

■ For more advanced students, make several copies of the description, cut the sentences apart and scramble them. Have students sequence the sentences and check the sequence against the versions in their notebooks.

Life Skills Reading

Focus: Students use real-life reading materials, and complete statements or answer questions with information found in the reading material.

Materials: Dictionaries; a class set of the selected Life Skills Reading activity sheet; appropriate realia, such as a form, sign, or label

Before class, look over the activity sheet and duplicate a class set. Copy the first sign, form, label, tag, or card from the activity sheet onto the board.

Preview Options

Show the realia to the class and elicit from students what they would expect to read on the item. For example, on a driver's license students might say "name" or "birthday."

Have students open their dictionaries to the page indicated on the activity sheet and ask questions about a sign, form, label, tag, or card that is similar to one presented in the reading. Ask Wh-questions about the item, such as "Where do you see this?" "Who reads this?" or "What is this for?"

For literacy level students, distribute the activity sheets and have students underline the words they know on each sign, form, label, tag, or card. Give students three to five minutes to accomplish this task. Then ask volunteers to spell words they know, while other students find them on the activity sheet. Continue until all the target words have been identified.

Presentation

Tell students that they will be reading different signs, forms, labels, tags, or cards to get specific information.

Use the item on the board as an example. Ask the class Wh-questions that point out the organization of the information in the example, such as "Where are the prices, on the right or on the left?" or "What information comes first, the name or the address?"

3. Copy the first question or fill-in-the-blank sentence onto the board. Get class consensus on the correct response.

Practice

4. Distribute the activity sheets and have students find and circle the words in the reading that are listed in the word box. Monitor student progress and go over students' work when they finish.

5. Have students silently scan the first item at the bottom of the activity sheet. Review the first item and, if necessary, follow the same procedure with the second item.

6. Have students work independently to complete the remaining items. Circulate and monitor student progress.

Follow-Up Options

■ Create additional questions about the reading material and write them on the board. Have students who complete the activity quickly write answers to the questions on the back of their activity sheets. Read the questions aloud with the entire class and have volunteers answer each one.

■ Ask students to bring in a sign, form, label, tag, or card similar to those shown on the activity sheet. Write four questions students can ask each other about the real-life reading. Pair students and have them take turns asking each other the questions.

Narrative Reading

Focus: Students make predictions about a reading passage, look up unfamiliar words in their dictionaries, and answer comprehension questions.

Materials: Dictionaries; a class set of the selected Narrative Reading activity sheets; Answer Cards; realia related to the selected reading

Before class, look over the activity sheet, taking note of the target vocabulary depicted. Collect the appropriate realia. Duplicate a class set of the activty sheet.

Preview Options

■ Ask three or four questions about the material on the activity sheet and the selected dictionary page.

■ Where appropriate, bring in an item or a picture of an item that relates to the reading topic. Ask questions to elicit student responses, such as "What is this used for?" or "When do you need this?"

Presentation

1. Tell students that they will be reading a short passage and answering questions about what they have read.

2. Distribute the activity sheets. Pair students and give them two minutes to talk about the picture at the top of the page. Have student volunteers share what they see with the class.

3. Use the picture to guide the class in making predictions about the content of the story.

4. Have students read the passage silently. When they have completed the reading, review the first item and come to consensus on the correct answer.

   For literacy level students, have students listen and follow along as you read the story and the items below the story.

Practice

5. Have students answer the items independently. Get class consensus on the correct responses. If students disagree on the correct answer, have them quote the part of the reading passage that verifies their answers.

   For literacy level students, read the story again. Then have them read along with you. Drop your voice and fade out if students can manage any of the story on their own. Read the first two items together and decide on the answers. Have students do the remaining questions with a partner. Discuss the answers.

Follow-Up Options

■ Have students talk about what they think will happen next in the story.

■ Create additional questions about the reading material and write them on the board. If possible, use a different kind of format than the one on the activity sheet. Have students who complete the activity quickly write answers to these questions on the back of their activity sheets. Read the questions aloud with the entire class and have volunteers answer each one.

A Activity Sheets for Using the Dictionary

* tapescript on p. 14

■ Look at My New Dictionary!
Focused Listening I / Dictionary, Contents /
(No Activity Sheet)

Look at the Contents pages in your dictionary.
Listen to the student talk about his new dictionary.
Point to the items you hear him talking about.

Look at my new dictionary! It's The **Basic Oxford Picture Dictionary.** And just look at these **Contents** pages. The contents pages have a lot of information.* I see **pictures,** and **unit numbers,** and **titles,** and **page numbers.** Hmmm... Unit I is called Everyday Language. I wonder what that means. There's a **picture** next to unit I. It's a picture of a pencil, a clock, and a dollar sign.* I don't want to learn about pencils. I'm looking for an apartment. Where can I find words that'll help me? Oh, here's a **picture of a house.** It's next to a unit called The Home. Unit number 4, The Home, starts on **page 22.*** How do I know which page to look at? There are so many pages. Oh, I see. Each dictionary page has **a title.** When I want to learn kitchen words, I just turn to **A Kitchen,** page 25.*

Hmmm... I see a lot of words on this Contents page that I don't know. Guess I'll look them up, one at a time. Let's see... **Seasons.** I don't know that word. **Seasons, page 4.** Seasons, seasons... yeah, here it is. Page 4. Oh... right! I understand. One word learned, only a hundred more to go!

■ Turn to Page 48
Focused Listening II / Activity Sheet, p. 15

Listen to the teachers. Check (✓) the title of the dictionary page.

1. Students, everyone look at page 48, **Basic Clothes.**

2. This week we're going to talk about going to the doctor. But first we need some vocabulary. Let's turn to pages 58 and 59, **The Body.**

3. Carlos, please tell me the page number for **Banking.** What page number is that? Right, thank you, page 70.

4. Our lesson today is on getting your car fixed. Class, please turn to page 77 in your dictionaries, **Parts of a Car.**

5. I want you to find the pictures and words for **Occupations and Workplaces.** They're on pages 82 through 83. There are many pages of Occupations, but only one page with Occupations and Workplaces.

■ Find the Word
Focused Listening II / Activity Sheet, p. 16

Listen to the teachers talking about the dictionary. Follow the directions on your paper.

1. Turn to page **48**, Basic Clothes. Find a word that starts with "u."

2. Turn to pages **58** and **59**, The Body. Find a word that ends with "w."

3. Open up to page **70**, Banking. Find a word that starts with "l."

4. Take a look at page **77**, Parts of a Car. Which word starts with "a"?

5. Turn to pages **82** and **83**, Occupations and Workplaces. Copy the word that ends with "c."

6. Let's look at pages **92** and **93**, Leisure. Find a sport that starts with "f."

7. Open your dictionaries to pages **2** and **3**, The ESL Classroom. Find a word that starts with "p."

8. Look at page **10**, Money. Find a word that ends with "t."

9. Everyone please open your books to page **6**. This page is called Times of Day. Which word starts with "a"?

10. It's time to look at the Appendix. Let's look at pages **96** and **97**. Look for the word that ends with "e."

■ **Listen to the teachers.**

■ **Check (✓) the title of the dictionary page.**

I.

7. **Clothes**	**48–57**
Basic Clothes ✓	48
Casual Clothes	49
Cold Weather Clothes	50
Underwear and Sleepwear	51
Describing Clothes	52
At the Store (Prepositions I)	54
Jewelry and Accessories	55
Taking Care of Clothes: The Laundromat	56
Taking Care of Clothes: The Tailor / Dry Cleaner	57

2.

8. **Health**	**58–67**
The Body	58
The Face and Head	60
Toiletries	61
Aches, Pains, and Injuries	62
Treatments	64
First Aid and Health Care Items	65
At a Medical Office	66

3.

9. **The Community**	**68–75**
The Community	68
Banking	70
The Post Office	71
An Intersection	72
Emergencies and Natural Disasters	74

4.

10. **Transportation**	**76–81**
Transportation	76
Parts of a Car	77
On the Road (Prepositions II)	78
At an Airport	80

5.

11. **Work**	**82–91**
Occupations and the Workplaces I	82
Occupations II	84
Occupations III	86
A Construction Site	87
At Work	88
A Day-Care Center	90

*tapescript on p. 14

Find the Word*

Focused Listening II/Teacher's Notes, p. 3/Dictionary, pp. 48, 58, 70, 77, 82–83, 92–93

■ **Fold your paper on the dotted line below.**
■ **Listen and write the page numbers.**

1.	Basic Clothes	page **48**	
2.	The Body	page _____	
3.	Banking	page _____	
4.	Parts of a Car	page _____	
5.	Occupations and Workplaces	pages _____	and _____
6.	Leisure	pages _____	and _____
7.	The ESL Classroom	pages _____	and _____
8.	Money	page _____	
9.	Time: Times of the Day	page _____	
10.	The World	pages _____	and _____

- FOLD HERE -

■ **Listen again and find the word.**
■ **Write the word below.**

1. **uniform**   2. _____

3. _____   4. _____

5. _____   6. _____

7. _____   8. _____

9. _____   10. _____

*tapescript on p. 14

TPR Sequence/Teacher's Notes, p. 4/Dictionary, pp. 104–120 (Index)

■ **Match the sentences to the pictures above.**

_____	Turn to page 86 and look for the word.	__I__	Read a sign "SALESPERSON WANTED."
_____	Find the word "salesperson."	_____	Look at picture 11. He's a salesperson.
_____	Turn to "S" in the index.	_____	Take out your dictionary.
_____	Find the page number next to "salesperson."	_____	You don't know one word: "salesperson."

1. ■ **Sit with a partner. Don't look at your partner's paper.**
   ■ **Ask your partner for the missing page numbers:**
      What page is _____ on?
   ■ **Write the missing page numbers on the Index.**

above [ə bŭv′]	54/1
accelerator [ăk sĕl′ə rā′tər]	__77__/13
Accessories [ăk sĕs′ə rēz]	55
accident [ăk′sə dənt]	____/4
accountant [ə kown′tənt]	86/9
Aches [āks]	62–63
across [ə krös′]	____/7
Activities, Indoor [īn′dör′ ăk tĭv′ə tēz]	93
Activities, Outdoor	
[owt′dör′ ăk tĭv′ə tēz]	92
actor [ăk′tər]	____/15
actress [ăk′trəs]	86/15
address [ă′drəs]	____/9
address, return [rə türn′ ə drĕs′]	71/7
adult [ə dŭlt′]	11/8
Africa [ă′frĭ kə]	____/2
afternoon [ăf′tər nōōn′]	6/2
Age [āj]	____
air conditioner [ër′ kən dĭ′shə nər]	26/4
Airport [ër′pört′]	80–81
aisle [ī′əl]	40/2
Alabama [ăl′ə bă′mə]	98/1

2. ■ **Listen to your partner's questions.**
   ■ **Look at the Index and answer the questions.**

1. ■ Sit with a partner. Don't look at your partner's paper.

   ■ Listen to your partner's questions.

   ■ Look at the Index and answer the questions.

above [ə bŭv′]	_____/1
accelerator [ăk sĕl′ə rā′tər]	**77** /13
Accessories [ăk sĕs′ə rēz]	55
accident [ăk′sə dənt]	74/4
accountant [ə kown′tənt]	86/9
Aches [āks]	_____
across [ə krös′]	79/7
Activities, Indoor [īn′dör′ ăk tĭv′ə tēz]	93
Activities, Outdoor	
[owt′dör′ ăk tĭv′ə tēz]	92
actor [ăk′tər]	86/15
actress [ăk′trəs]	86/15
address [ă′drəs]	71/9
address, return [rə türn′ ə drĕs′]	71/7
adult [ə dŭlt′]	_____/8
Africa [ă′frĭ kə]	96/2
afternoon [ăf′tər nōōn′]	_____/2
Age [āj]	13
air conditioner [ër′ kən dĭ′shə nər]	26/4
Airport [ër′pört′]	_____
aisle [ī′əl]	40/2
Alabama [ăl′ə bă′mə]	_____/1

2. ■ Ask your partner for the missing page numbers.

   What page is _____ *on?*

   ■ Write the missing page numbers on the Index.

■ **Find these pictures in your dictionary.**

a notebook	long hair	a baseball cap
glasses	a Band-Aid	a car

■ **Walk around the room. Ask and answer this question:**
   Do you have _____ ?

■ **Write a different name on each line.**

Yes _____

No _____

Yes _____

No _____

Yes _____

No _____

Yes _____

No _____

Yes _____

No _____

Yes _____

No _____

Board Game/Teacher's Notes, p. 8/Dictionary, all pages

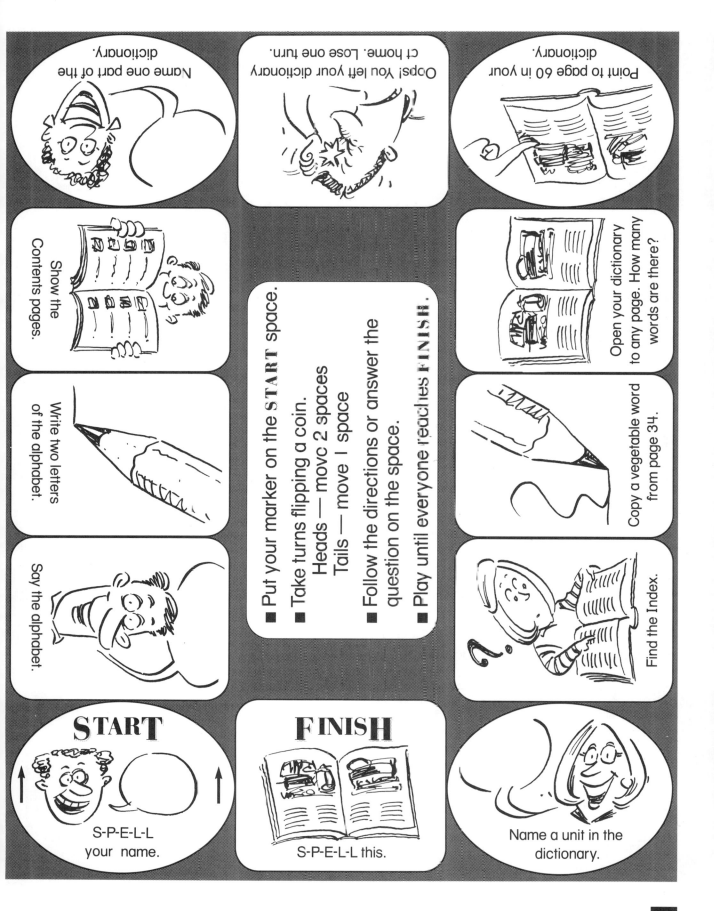

Name one part of the dictionary.

Oops! You left your dictionary ct home. Lose one turn.

Point to page 60 in your dictionary.

Show the Contents pages.

Open your dictionary to any page. How many words are there?

Write two letters of the alphabet.

- Put your marker on the **START** space.
- Take turns flipping a coin.
  Heads — move 2 spaces
  Tails — move 1 space
- Follow the directions or answer the question on the space.
- Play until everyone reaches **FINISH**.

Copy a vegetable word from page 34.

Say the alphabet.

Find the Index.

START

S-P-E-L-L your name.

FINISH

S-P-E-L-L this.

Name a unit in the dictionary.

Make a Picture Alphabet

LEA Project/Teacher's Notes, p. 10/Alphabet Cards, pp. 172–173

THE PROJECT:

■ **You are going to make a picture alphabet with three other classmates.**

■ **Then you will talk, write, and read about the experience.**

DIRECTIONS:

1. Sit with three other students.
   Learn each other's names.

2. Get some <u>old magazines</u>, a <u>large sheet of paper</u>,
   some <u>scissors</u>, and some <u>glue</u> or <u>tape</u> from your teacher.

3. Write the alphabet on the large sheet of paper.
   Leave space under each letter to put a picture.

4. Look in the magazines for pictures that you can name in English.
   Find a picture for the letter A. Cut it out.
   Cut out pictures for each letter of the alphabet.

5. Put the pictures in alphabetical order.
   Glue or tape the pictures under the letters on your paper.

6. Look for the words in the Index of your dictionary.
   Write the words on the paper under your pictures.

7. Put your group's paper on the board.
   Show your words to the class.

8. Tell your teacher how to make picture alphabets.
   (Your teacher will write what you say on the board.)

9. Look at the sentences on the board and copy them.

10. Read the sentences to a classmate.

The Contents

■ **Read the Contents page below.**

■ **Circle these words:**

| Airport | Appendix | Index | Recreation | Work |

■ **Write the missing words or numbers.**

1. Unit _12_ is about ___Recreation___ .

2. The Appendix starts on page _____ .

3. Airport words are on pages _____ and _____ .

4. The Index begins on page _____ .

5. Unit _____ shows many different Occupations.

Pavi sees an ad, "All Toiletries on Sale Today". She does not understand the word "Toiletries." Her friends do not know it. Pavi decides to use her picture dictionary. She looks in the Index under T. Toiletries are on page 61.

Pavi turns to page 61 and looks at the pictures. Toiletries are shampoo, soap, toothpaste, and deodorant. She needs some shampoo. She is going to Rex's Drugstore today to buy some shampoo on sale.

■ **Circle the answer.**

1. Pavi has a picture dictionary.   (Yes)   No

2. She wants to find the word "Toiletries."   Yes   No

3. She finds the word in the Appendix.   Yes   No

4. Pavi looks at the pictures of toiletries.   Yes   No

5. Toiletries are things to put in the toilet.   Yes   No

6. Soap is on sale today at Rex's Drugstore.   Yes   No

I Activity Sheets for Everyday Language

* tapescript on p. 26

Unit 1 Everyday Language Tapescripts

■ Day by Day
Focused Listening I / Dictionary, p.5
(No Activity Sheet)

Look at page 5 in your dictionary. Listen to Max Rosentreader talk about his calendar. Point to the days you hear him talking about.

Ah, let's see. **Today** is the sixth, **Wednesday**. What's on TV tonight? Nothing?! Typical! a new year and nothing's on TV!* There wasn't anything on **yesterday** either. Yesterday the TV shows were terrible.* I love to watch TV at night. Sometimes I have to work late like **tomorrow**. Oh, I hate working late on **Thursdays**. I miss all my shows.* Of course, last **Friday** was great. Parades and football all day. I love to watch TV on the **first** of January.* Oh, good! Something's coming on at 9:00.

(Click) NO!... No picture! No sound! The TV's broken! Good thing I'm taking a TV repair class. We started on the **second** of January and we meet every **Saturday** morning.* I hope I can fix this TV soon. Next **Tuesday**, the twelfth. I have a date with Lyla. We're planning to watch an old romantic movie together. Gee, I'd better call on **Monday** and remind her!* Of course, I never make plans for **Sunday** nights. The best animal shows are on Sunday.*

Now, when is mom's birthday, next week or the week after? I think it's the eleventh, **Monday**. Yes, I'm sure it's next Monday. I'll call her between the news and the gameshows. Ah! It's working now. Don't you think TV repair is the perfect occupation for me?

■ A Colorful Classroom
Focused Listening II / Activity Sheet, p. 27

Listen to the people talking about classroom items. Follow the directions on your paper.

1. Please get me the **yellow pencil** on the desk.
   This pencil?
   No, the yellow one.
2. Can I have the **red book**, please?
   This book?
   No, the red one.
3. Let me see that **purple pen**.
   Here it is. Why do you want it?
   I love purple things!
4. Sit down on that **black chair** over there.
   The black chair?
   Yes, the one next to the computer.
5. I'm looking for my **orange notebook**.
   I see an orange notebook over there, on that desk.
   Oh yes, there it is.
6. I need a piece of **white chalk**.
   What color?
   White. It's a good color for this chalkboard.
7. Where's the teacher in this class?
   She's the woman dressed in **blue**.
   Oh, I see her. What a pretty blue blouse.

■ Nickels and Dimes
Focused Listening II / Activity Sheet, p. 28

Listen to the conversations. Circle the letter under the picture.

1. I need to make a phone call. Do you have change?
   Sure, here are two **dimes**.
2. Go buy a newspaper.
   Do you have a **quarter**?
   Yeah, here ya' go.
3. Could I have a **dollar** please?
   Why? What can you buy with a dollar?
   I'm going to buy a lottery ticket.
4. Do you want a piece of gum?
   Sure!
   Okay, give me a **nickel** and I can buy some.
5. Could we have our **check** please?
   Sure. You can pay the check up at the counter.
   Thank you.
6. How will you be paying for that today?
   Let's see. Can I use my **credit card**?
   Yes, we take all major credit cards.

- **Fold the paper on the dotted line.**
- **Listen to the people talking about classroom items.**
- **Circle the item they need.**

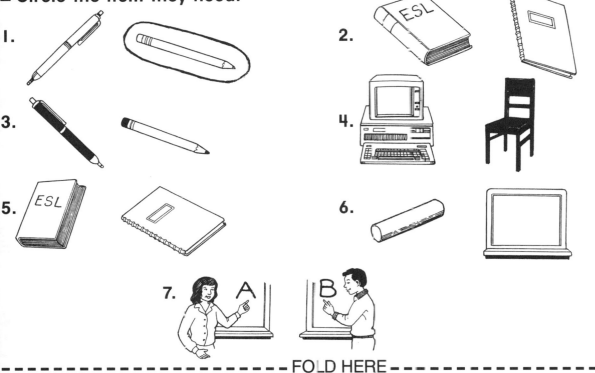

1.

2.

3.

4.

5.

6.

7.

- FOLD HERE -

- **Listen again to the people talking about the classroom items.**
- **Make a check (✔) under the correct color.**

	black	blue	orange	purple	red	white	yellow
1.							✔
2.							
3.							
4.							
5.							
6.							
7.							

*tapescript on p. 26

■ **Listen to the conversations.**
■ **Circle the letter under the picture.**

1.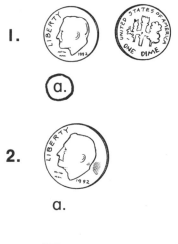

     ⓐ   b.

2.

     a.   b.

3.

     a.   b.

4.

     a.   b.

5.

Bud's Burgers
chicken	6.50
coke	1.00
Sub Total	7.50
Tax	.62
Total	8.12

Peter's Plumbing
parts 17.00
labor 57.00
total 69.00

     a.   b.

6.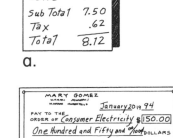

     a.   b.

*tapescript on p. 26

Sit Down and Study

TPR Sequence/Teacher's Notes, p. 4/Dictionary, pp. 2–3

■ Match the sentences to the pictures above.

_____ Stand up and stretch.	_____ Write in your notebook.
_____ Look at the clock.	__1__ Sit down at your desk.
_____ Close your notebook.	_____ Pick up your pencil.
_____ Open your notebook.	_____ Look out the window.

How's the Weather?

Info Exchange/Teachers' Notes, p. 5/Dictionary, p. 8

I. ■ **Sit with a partner. Don't look at your partner's paper.**
■ **Look at your weather map.**
■ **Tell your partner about the weather in:**
   Seattle, New York, Chicago, Miami.

2. ■ **Listen to the weather in:**
   Seattle, Los Angeles, Denver, Houston.
■ **Make a check (✔) under the weather on your chart.**

	sunny	cloudy	raining	windy	hot	warm	cold	cool
Seattle			✔				✔	
Los Angeles								
Denver								
Houston								

I. ■ **Sit with a partner. Don't look at your partner's paper.**
■ **Listen to the weather in:**

   Seattle, New York, Chicago, Miami.

■ **Make a check (✓) under the weather on your chart.**

	sunny	cloudy	raining	windy	hot	warm	cold	cool
Seattle			✔				✔	
New York								
Chicago								
Miami								

2. ■ **Look at your weather map.**
■ **Tell your partner about the weather in:**

   Seattle, Los Angeles, Denver, Houston.

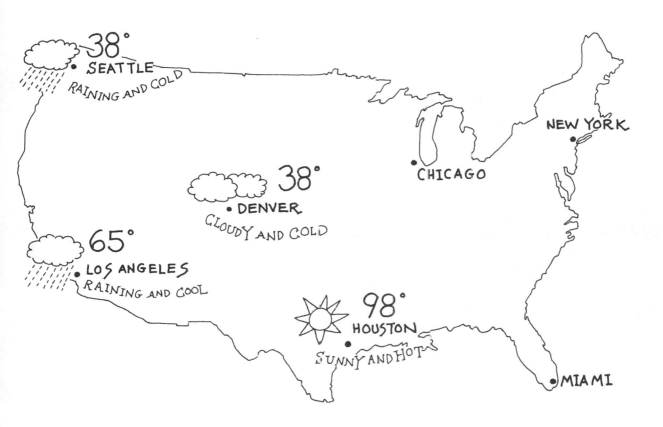

Mixer/Teacher's Notes, p. 6/Dictionary, p. 5

■ **Write the missing letters in the months.**

■ **Walk around the room. Ask and answer this question:**
   When is your birthday?

■ **Write a different name in each box.**

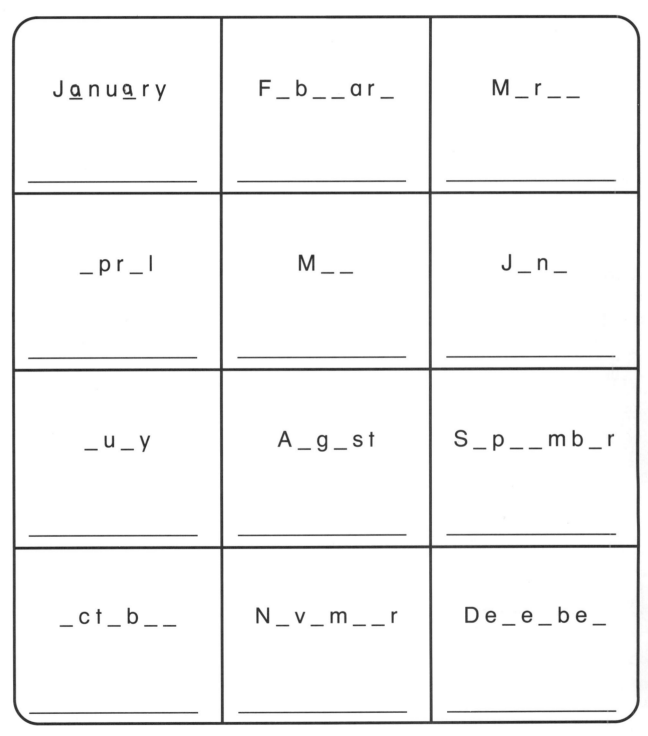

J a n u a r y _____	F _ b _ _ a r _ _____	M _ r _ _ _____
_ p r _ l _____	M _ _ _____	J _ n _ _____
_ u _ y _____	A _ g _ s t _____	S _ p _ _ m b _ r _____
_ c t _ b _ _ _____	N _ v _ m _ _ r _____	D e _ e _ b e _ _____

Everyday Language

Board Game/Teacher's Notes, p. 8/Dictionary, pp. 2–7

When's your birthday?

How much money do you have today?

What's your **favorite** color?

Draw a black circle.

S-P-E-L-L this.

Put your marker on the **START** space.

Take turns flipping a coin.
Heads — move 2 spaces
Tails — move 1 space

Follow the directions or answer the question on the space.

Play until everyone reaches **FINISH**.

Open a book.

What time is it?

SHOW US!

Name something in the classroom.

What's your favorite season?

START

Say your name.

FINISH

Point to something green.

What day is it today?

Unit 1/Everyday Language   **33**

Design a Classroom

THE PROJECT:

■ **Your teacher is going to put a <u>large sheet of butcher paper</u> on the wall and draw walls on the paper like this.**

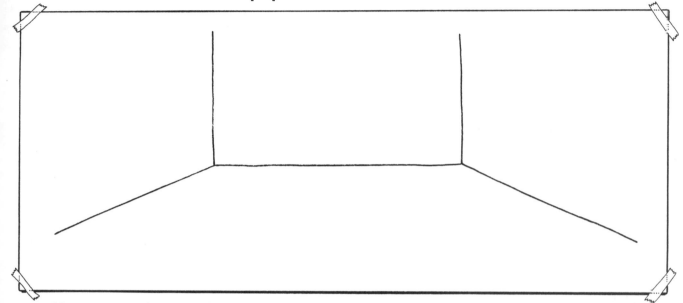

■ **You are going to design a new classroom on the paper.**
  Then you will talk, write, and read about this new classroom.

DIRECTIONS:

1. Get <u>colored markers</u>, <u>paper</u>, <u>tape</u> and <u>scissors</u> from your teacher.

2. Choose one item in the classroom and draw it.

a book	a computer	a television
a chair	a desk	a table
a chalkboard	a plant	a teacher
a clock	a student	a window

3. Cut out your picture and put tape on the back.

4. Decide with your classmates where to tape your picture on the paper.

5. Describe the new classroom.
   (Your teacher will write what you say on the board.)

6. Look at the sentences on the board and copy them.

7. Read the sentences to a classmate.

Life Skills Reading/Teacher's Notes, p. 11/Dictionary, p. 10 and p. 70

■ **Read the bill.**

■ **Circle these words:**

amount	date	payment

☎	Account Number	818 990 5500 947 S 9066	page 1
	Statement Date	Jan 14, 1994	

Account Summary	Previous bill		31.19	
	Payment	12/8	31.19 CR	
	Balance ***Thank you for your payment***			.00
	Current Charges:			
	Pacific Bell (Page 4)		10.38	
	Long Distance Dec. (Page 5)		15.00	
				25.38
	Total amount due by Feb. 14, 1994			25.38

■ **Write the missing words.**

1. The _____ is from the telephone company.

2. The _____ is 1/14/94.

3. The _____ of the bill is $25.38.

■ **Look at the check and follow the directions.**

1. Write today's date on the check.

2. Write the missing words in the amount.

3. Sign your name.

ABCDEFGHIJK
PQRSTUVWXYZ
ABCDEFGHIJKL

DATE _____

PAY TO *Pacific Bell*   **$25.38**

and 38/100———— DOLLARS

_____

154320784123

A Very Busy Morning

Narrative Reading/Teacher's Notes, p. 12/Dictionary, pp. 2–7

Today is Monday, September 18. It's 8:00 in the morning on the first day of school. This morning is a very busy time for Bertha Diaz. Bertha is talking on the phone and writing on the calendar. She is a teacher. Her son, Ramon, is pointing to the clock. Her daughter, Eva, is looking at her watch. They are late for school. Bertha is always busy, but this morning is terrible!

Bertha's favorite month is July. In July, Bertha doesn't teach. Her children don't go to school, and no one in the family looks at a watch or a calendar!

■ Circle the answer.

1. Is it Monday?	(Yes)	No
2. Is it afternoon?	Yes	No
3. Is it 8:00 p.m.?	Yes	No
4. Is it June?	Yes	No
5. Is Bertha a teacher?	Yes	No
6. Is Eva looking at the clock?	Yes	No

2 Activity Sheets for People

Hair by Paulo

Focused Listening I / Dictionary, p. 13
(No Activity Sheet)

Look at page 13 in your dictionary. Listen to Paulo, the world famous hairdresser, talk about his customers. Point to the hairstyles he describes.

Come in! Come in! I am Paulo. You want a new look, yes? I believe it is very important to change your look. These old pictures of me will show you how much a person can change! Here's a picture of me with a **beard**. I liked that beard, short but elegant.* Now, here I am with only my **mustache**. A different look to be sure, but still very much me.* But we need to talk about you and your hair. So many styles to choose from....How do you feel about long and straight? Here's a picture of Sue Lee when she came to me last year. Her **long** black hair was so straight and beautiful.* Of course now I can show you the picture after my fabulous cut. Straight yes, but **short**, short short! What do you think? What am I thinking!! Of course, this is too short for you.* What do you think about curls? Here's a picture of Doris, my model, in her blond wig. Her hair is very **curly**. Curls are not your style. I see...* Do you like waves? Soft waves on medium length hair? Here's Doris in a **wavy** blond wig. I think this would be perfect for you. No? (sigh)* All right then. Maybe just a shampoo. No cutting. We'll keep your hair the way it is. Like this picture of Doris, **straight**, nothing fancy.* But what about a little color? Maybe red, like my assistant Jule's **red** hair. (Jule's hair is actually **gray**, but he changes his hair color every week.* Last week his hair was **brown**!*) You like red? Fantastic.* Go with Ben. He's the gentleman with no hair, the **bald** man, see him? He'll take you to the dressing room. No, no, don't thank me. This is what I live for.

Is That Her?!

Focused Listening II / Activity Sheet, p. 39

Listen to George describe different people. Follow the directions on your paper.

1. You know? I can't wait to meet your new girlfriend. What's her name again? Helen? There's a woman walking toward us. Her hair is **dark** and **wavy**. She's **short** and very attractive. Is that her? No?

2. I see a woman over there, on the bench. She's a little **heavy** and her hair is **short** and **curly**. Is that her? Oh, I guess not.

3. I see a **thin** woman with **short wavy** hair. She's standing next to the **tall** man? Is that her? Oh, right. She is very **young**.

4. Oh, oh! Look on the other side of the **tall** man. See that woman? She's about 24 and her hair is **blond, long,** and **straight**. Is that her? No??!!

5. Okay, look over there at that woman. She's next to the man with the **mustache**. She isn't **short**, and she isn't **thin**. Her hair isn't **blond** and she isn't a **teenager**. See her? Her eyes are very **large**. Is that her? It is?!!! Wow! She's beautiful!

Maya Petrov's Day

Focused Listening II / Activity Sheet, p. 40

Listen to Maya talk about her day. Make an X in the correct box.

1. I'm Maya Petrov. I'm really busy right now, but I can tell you my schedule if you want to hear it. I **get up** at 7:00, while my husband, Boris, is still sleeping.

2. Then at 7:30 I **take** a nice, hot **shower**, but only for a few minutes. We can't use too much water.

3. I **leave the house** for work at 8:30. I have to go to work from 9:00 to 5:00.

4. At 6:30 I go to school. My English teacher is a very nice, tall man. I **study** hard in that class.

5. At 10:00 I **go to bed**, but I don't **go to sleep**. I like to watch the news on TV.

6. By 11:30, Boris, my husband, kisses me goodnight and we **go to sleep**. I'm so tired, I usually go to sleep right away. (yawn) Oh, excuse me!

Is That Her?!*

■ **Listen to George describe different people.**
■ **Write the numbers under the correct pictures.**

------------------- FOLD HERE -------------------

■ **Fold the paper in half.**
■ **Listen again and circle the correct words.**
■ **Unfold the paper and check your answers.**

1. Woman #1 has   short   hair.
                      (dark)

2. Woman #2 is   a little heavy.
                   short.

3. Woman #3 is   tall   and young.
                   thin

4. Woman #4 has   long,   blond hair.
                   short,

5. Woman #5 has   small,   beautiful eyes.
                   large,

  * tapescript on p. 38

■ **Listen to Maya talk about her day.**
■ **Make an X in the correct box.**

1.

☐ ☒

2.

☐ ☐

3.

☐ ☐

4.

☐ ☐

5.

☐ ☐

6.

☐ ☐

* tapescript on p. 38

Coming Home

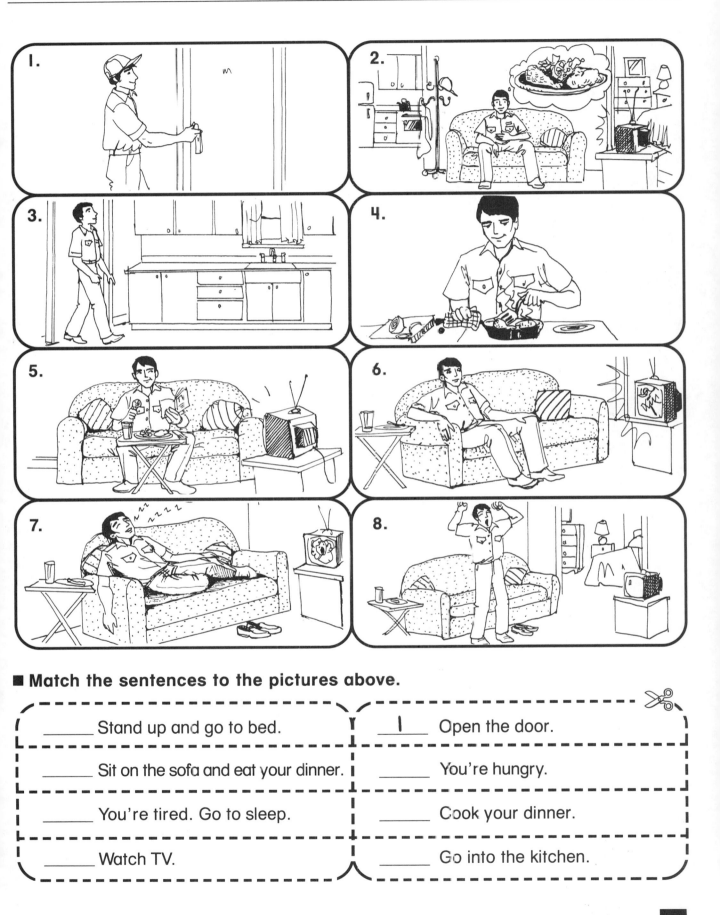

■ **Match the sentences to the pictures above.**

_____ Stand up and go to bed.

___I___ Open the door.

_____ Sit on the sofa and eat your dinner.

_____ You're hungry.

_____ You're tired. Go to sleep.

_____ Cook your dinner.

_____ Watch TV.

_____ Go into the kitchen.

Describe Me

1. ■ Sit with a partner. Don't look at your partner's paper.
   ■ Look at the pictures of Mario and Sara.
   ■ Describe Mario and Sara to your partner.

Mario   Sara

2. ■ Listen to your partner describe Harry and Kim.
   ■ Circle the description you hear.

Harry is	short. average height. tall.		Kim is	short. average height. tall.
Harry is	thin. average weight. heavy.		Kim is	thin average weight. heavy.
Harry has	straight wavy hair. curly		Kim has	straight wavy hair. curly

1. ■ **Sit with a partner. Don't look at your partner's paper.**
   ■ **Listen to your partner describe Mario and Sara.**
   ■ **Circle the description you hear.**

Mario is	short. average height. tall.
Mario is	thin. average weight. heavy.
Mario has	straight wavy hair. curly

Sara is	short. average height. tall.
Sara is	thin average weight. heavy.
Sara has	straight wavy hair. curly

2. ■ **Look at the pictures of Harry and Kim.**
   ■ **Describe Harry and Kim to your partner.**

Harry   Kim

Getting to Know You

Mixer/Teacher's Notes, p. 6/Dictionary, pp. 14–15

■ **Write the missing words in the questions.**
■ **Walk around the room. Ask and answer the questions.**
■ **Write a different name in each box.**

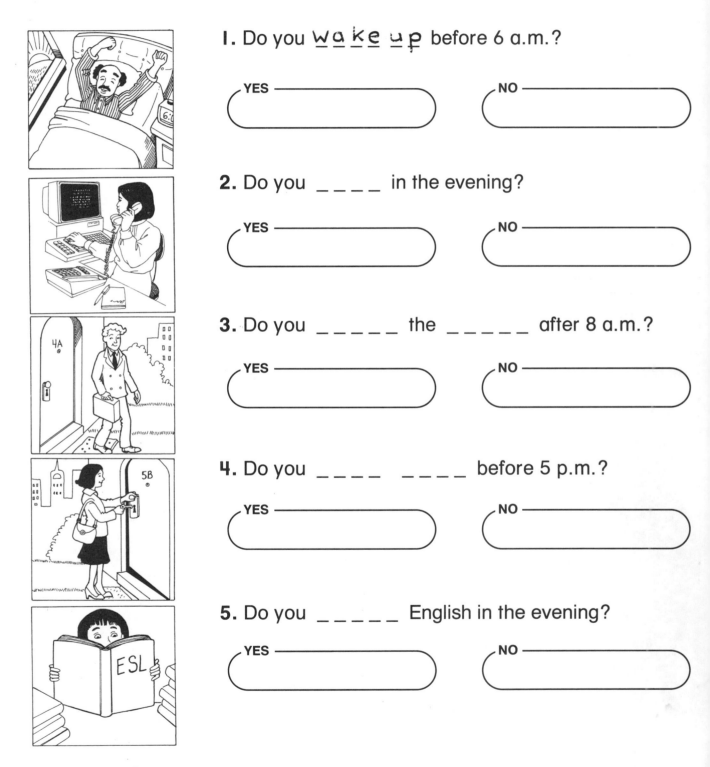

1. Do you w͟a͟ k͟e͟ u͟p͟ before 6 a.m.?

YES ——— NO ———

2. Do you _ _ _ _ in the evening?

YES ——— NO ———

3. Do you _ _ _ _ _ _ the _ _ _ _ _ _ after 8 a.m.?

YES ——— NO ———

4. Do you _ _ _ _ _ _ _ _ before 5 p.m.?

YES ——— NO ———

5. Do you _ _ _ _ _ _ English in the evening?

YES ——— NO ———

Board Game/Teacher's Notes, p. 8/Dictionary, pp. 11–15

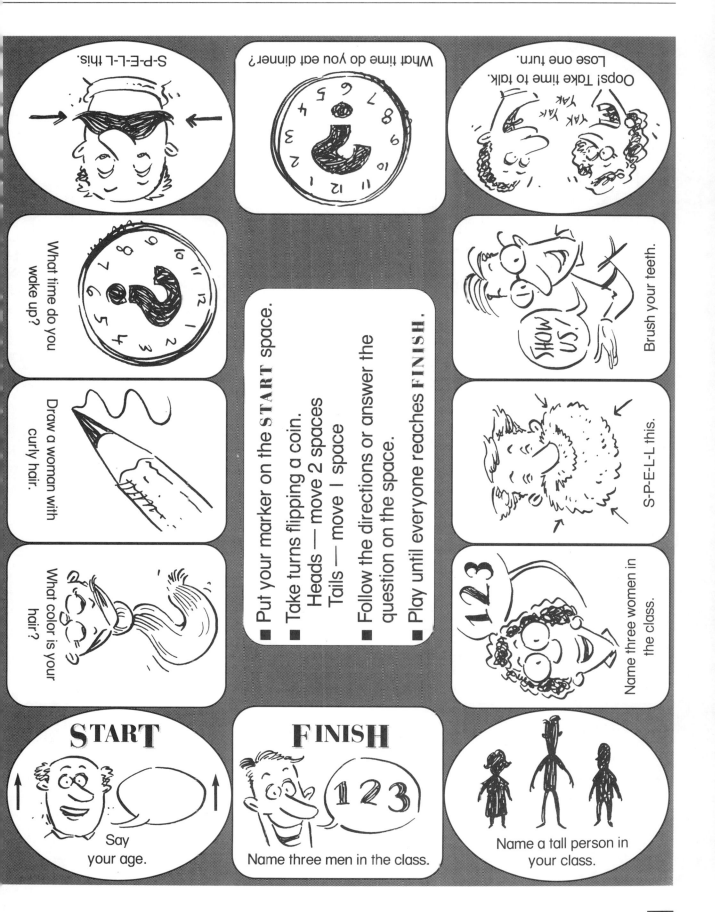

S-P-E-L-L this.

What time do you eat dinner?

Oops! Take time to talk.
Lose one turn.

What time do you wake up?

Brush your teeth.

SHOW US!

Draw a woman with curly hair.

- Put your marker on the **START** space.
- Take turns flipping a coin.
  Heads — move 2 spaces
  Tails — move 1 space
- Follow the directions or answer the question on the space.
- Play until everyone reaches **FINISH**.

S-P-E-L-L this.

What color is your hair?

123

Name three women in the class.

START

Say your age.

FINISH

123

Name three men in the class.

Name a tall person in your class.

LEA Picture/Teacher's Notes, p. 9/Dictionary, pp. 12–13

■ **Look at the picture.**
■ **Describe the burglars.**

■ **Copy the description.**

_____

_____

_____

_____

_____

_____

_____

Life Skills Reading/Teacher's Notes, p. 11/Dictionary, pp. 11–12

■ Circle these words:

| adult child height maximum minimum weight |

PLEASE READ BEFORE ENTERING THIS AREA

Maximum Height = 6'6"
Minimum Height = 4'

Maximum Weight = 200 pounds
Minimum Weight = 50 pounds

NO EXCEPTIONS

PAY ONE PRICE • RIDE ALL DAY
TICKET PRICES
Adult $5.00
Senior Citizen $3.00
Student (13-18 or with i.d.) $2.50
Child 2-12 $1.75

■ Write the missing information.

1. The ticket for an adult is __$5.00__ .

2. The ticket for a child is $_____ .

3. The ticket for a teenager is $_____ .

4. The minimum height for this ride is _____ ' _____ ".

5. The maximum height for this ride is _____ ' _____ ".

6. The maximum weight for this ride is _____ lbs.

7. The minimum weight for this ride is _____ lbs.

Mary, Is That You?

Narrative Reading/Teacher's Notes, p. 12/Dictionary, pp. 14—15

Mary and Phil are married, but they don't see each other very much. Usually Phil wakes up at 4:00 in the morning. He takes a shower and shaves. He leaves the house at 5:00 a.m. He doesn't eat breakfast at home because he works in a hospital cafeteria. He comes home at 4:00 in the afternoon and goes to bed by 8:30.

Mary usually wakes up at 7:00 in the morning. She cooks breakfast, eats, and gets dressed. She cooks dinner in the morning and puts it in the refrigerator. She leaves the house at 12:00 noon. Mary works in a factory and she comes home at 9:30 in the evening. After work she takes a shower, brushes her teeth, and watches TV. She goes to bed at 11:00.

Mary and Phil like the weekends. On Saturday and Sunday they can go to bed and wake up at the same time.

■ Circle the answer.

1. Who wakes up first?   Mary   (Phil)

2. Who shaves?   Mary   Phil

3. Who leaves the house first?   Mary   Phil

4. Who works in a hospital?   Mary   Phil

5. Who works in a factory?   Mary   Phil

3 Activity Sheets for Family

* tapescript on p. 50

Unit 3 Family Tapescripts

■ Today Is Josh's Birthday
Focused Listening I / Dictionary, p. 17
(No Activity Sheet)

Look at page 17 in your dictionary. Listen to Josh's grandmother at Josh's birthday party. Point to the pictures she is talking about.

      I just love birthday parties. Okay, everyone, let's get started! Come into the dining room. Aunt Rhonda, play your guitar and **sing "Happy Birthday."** Wait, Rhonda, don't sing until everyone is here. Your voice is so beautiful.* I see that Neil is ready with his camera. Come on Neil, **take a picture**. You always take good pictures.* Now we can **blow out the candles**. Okay, Josh, we're ready. Blow out the candles! Blow out all of them.* Let's **cut the cake**. Cut big pieces, Rhonda, we all love birthday cake.* Anybody want coffee? Not you, Jonathan! You're too young. You **drink milk** today. Here, have a big glass.* Josh, **open a card** and read it. I'm so proud of the way you read.* Oh, look at Andy **kiss** Sally. Sally is his first child. Neil, can you get a picture of Andy kissing her?* Hey, Josh—I think Anya wants to **give a present** to you. She always gives you something special. I wonder what it is?* Oh, everyone is having such a good time! Why, just look at my Phil **laugh**. Phil, what are you laughing about? Something Eli said, I bet.* Now, Eli, I know why you're smiling. You should **smile**. Tomorrow is your birthday! Okay, everyone, don't eat too much birthday cake. Tomorrow we're going to have another birthday party—for Eli!

■ Guest List
Focused Listening II / Activity Sheet, p. 51

Listen to the woman talk about her guest list. Follow the directions on your paper.

1. Honey, I think the party's all set. My **grandparents** are coming. Grandma Rose will be pushing Grandpa Harry in his wheelchair. They'll be here at 6:00, or maybe earlier.

2. Of course my **Aunt** Rhonda is coming. Aunt Rhonda always brings her fruit salad.

3. **Uncle** Louie can't come. His boss is retiring and he's going to that party.

4. Of course, my **mom** and **dad** can come. Pearl is making the cake like she always does and Alex is bringing the camera to take pictures.

5. My **sister** Rita can come. She hates parties, but she loves Ralph.

6. My **niece** Patty is coming with my sister. She loves to wear her party clothes as much as she can.

7. My **nephew** David can't come. He's sick with the flu and has to stay in bed.

8. Don't forget my **brother**. Of course, he can come. It's his birthday!! Ralph always comes to his own birthday party.

■ How Do They Feel?
Focused Listening II / Activity Sheet, p. 52

Listen and follow the directions on your paper.

1. Where's my drink? I'm so **thirsty**. Waiter, I need a glass of water, please.

2. Oh, my goodness! Mandy, what a lovely present. I'm so **surprised**. I'm going to put it on right now.

3. I miss my family. My sister sent this picture. It makes me **homesick**. I really want to see her.

4. Mommy, I'm **bored**. I want to go outside. There's nothing for me to do. I wish Bruno would come over.

5. Honey, I'm going to lie down. I've had a hard day and I'm really **tired**.

6. Look! Look! Look what you did!! Do you see? That makes me **angry**.

7. I want the doctor to hurry. I'm going to be **nervous** until I hear about my test.

8. Eli hit a homerun! Eli hit a homerun! I'm **excited**, Alex, aren't you?

9. Who's my little sweet thing? Who's my **happy** bunny? Who's my love? Natalie, that's who!

■ **Fold your paper on the dotted line.**
■ **Listen and number the people in the order they are named.**

___ mom and dad   _1_ grandparents   ___ brother   ___ sister

___ aunt   ___ uncle   ___ niece   ___ nephew

- FOLD HERE -

■ **Listen and check (✔) the correct answer.**

		Can come	Can't come
	grandparents	✓	
◯	aunt		
	uncle		
	mother		
	father		
	sister		
	niece		
	nephew		
◯	brother		

* tapescript on p. 50

■ Listen and write the correct number on the line.

a. _____

b. _____

c. _____

d. _____

e. _____

f. _____

g. _____

h. _____

i. _____

* tapescript on p. 50

Make a Birthday Card

TPR Sequence/Teacher's Notes, p. 4/Dictionary, p. 17

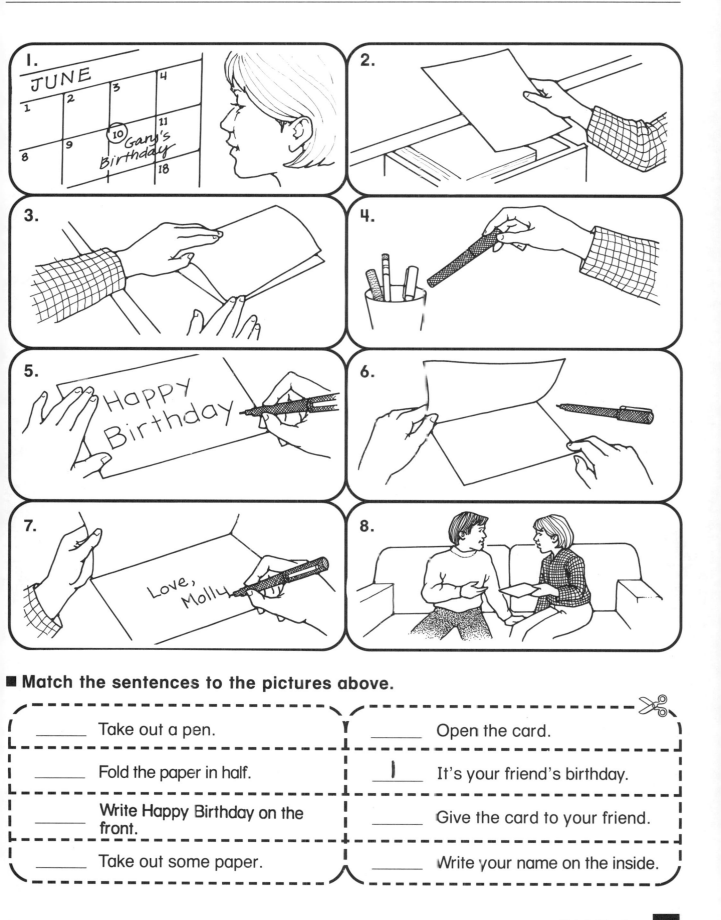

■ Match the sentences to the pictures above.

_____ Take out a pen.	_____ Open the card.
_____ Fold the paper in half.	___I___ It's your friend's birthday.
_____ Write Happy Birthday on the front.	_____ Give the card to your friend.
_____ Take out some paper.	_____ Write your name on the inside.

Unit 3/Family **53**

1. ■ Sit with a partner. Don't look at your partner's paper.
   ■ Tell your partner what these people are doing:
   Tom   Rick   Tim   Nora

2. ■ Listen to your partner.
   ■ Write these names in the correct spaces.
   Bob   Leo   Sandy   Flor

I. ■ **Sit with a partner. Don't look at your partner's paper.**

■ **Listen to your partner.**

■ **Write these names in the correct spaces:**

   Tom   Rick   Tim   Nora

2. ■ **Tell your partner what these people are doing:**

   Bob   Leo   Sandy   Flor

Who Lives in Your House?

Mixer/Teacher's Notes, p. 6/Dictionary, p. 16

- **Write the missing letters in the words.**
- **Walk around the room. Ask and answer this question:**
  Do you live with your__________?
- **Write a different name in each box.**

1. Do you live with your s i s t e r ?

YES

NO

2. Do you live with your b r _ t h _ _ ?

YES

NO

3. Do you live with your g r _ _ _ p a _ e _ _ s?

YES

NO

4. Do you live with your w _ _ e or _ u s b _ _ d?

YES

NO

5. Do you live with your a _ n _ or u _ c _ _ ?

YES

NO

Family

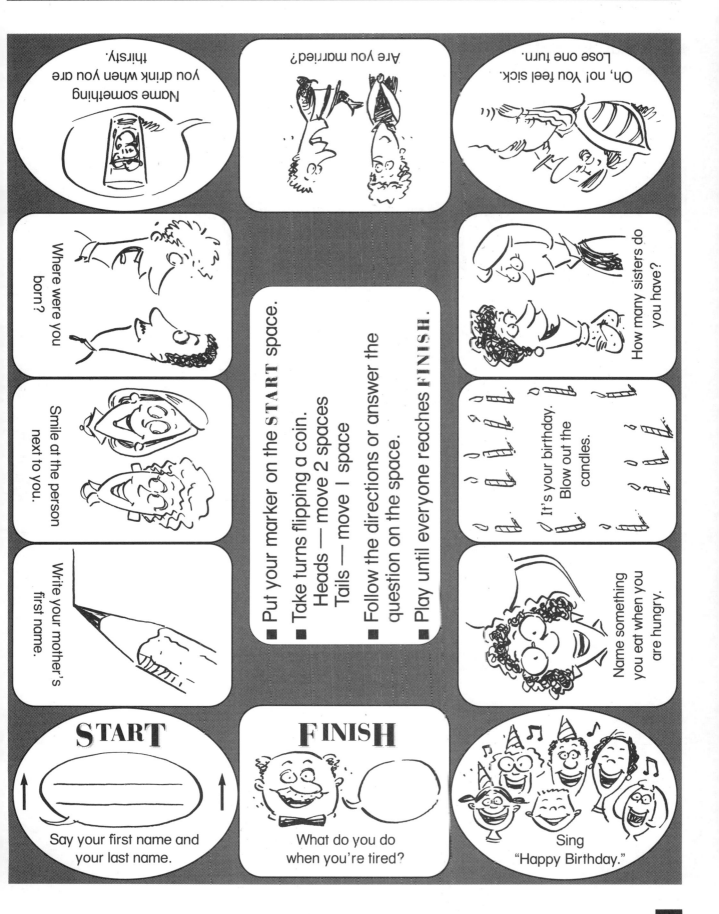

Name something you drink when you are thirsty.

Are you married?

Oh, no! You feel sick. Lose one turn.

Where were you born?

How many sisters do you have?

- Put your marker on the **START** space.
- Take turns flipping a coin.
  Heads — move 2 spaces
  Tails — move 1 space
- Follow the directions or answer the question on the space.
- Play until everyone reaches **FINISH**.

Smile at the person next to you.

It's your birthday. Blow out the candles.

Write your mother's first name.

Name something you eat when you are hungry.

START

Say your first name and your last name.

FINISH

What do you do when you're tired?

Sing "Happy Birthday."

■ **Look at the pictures.**
■ **Describe the situation to your teacher.**

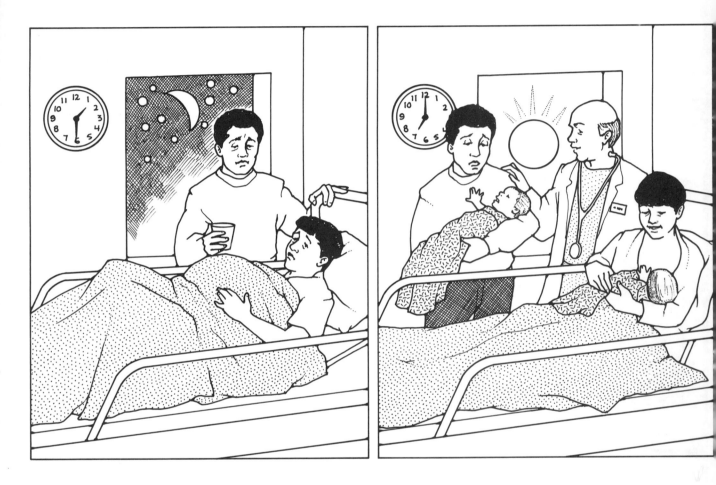

■ **Copy the description.**

_____

_____

_____

_____

_____

_____

_____

Life Skills Reading/Teacher's Notes, p. 11/Dictionary, pp. 20–21

■ **Read the greeting cards.**

■ **Circle these words:**

retire	sad	baby	sick

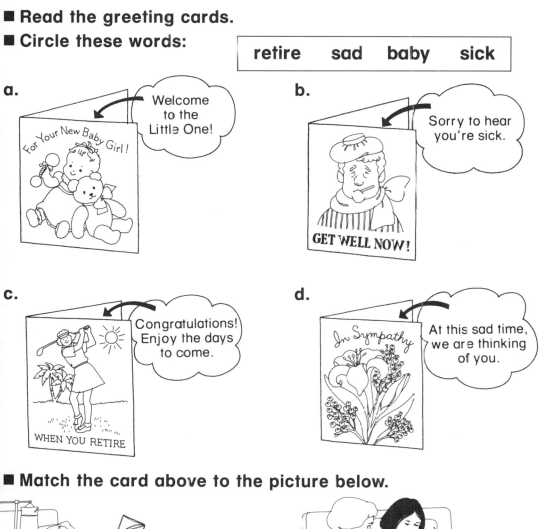

a.
For Your New Baby Girl!

Welcome to the Little One!

b.
GET WELL NOW!

Sorry to hear you're sick.

c.
WHEN YOU RETIRE

Congratulations! Enjoy the days to come.

d.
In Sympathy

At this sad time, we are thinking of you.

■ **Match the card above to the picture below.**

1. _____

2. _____

3. _____

4. _____

Narrative Reading/Teacher's Notes, p. 12/Dictionary, pp. 16–21

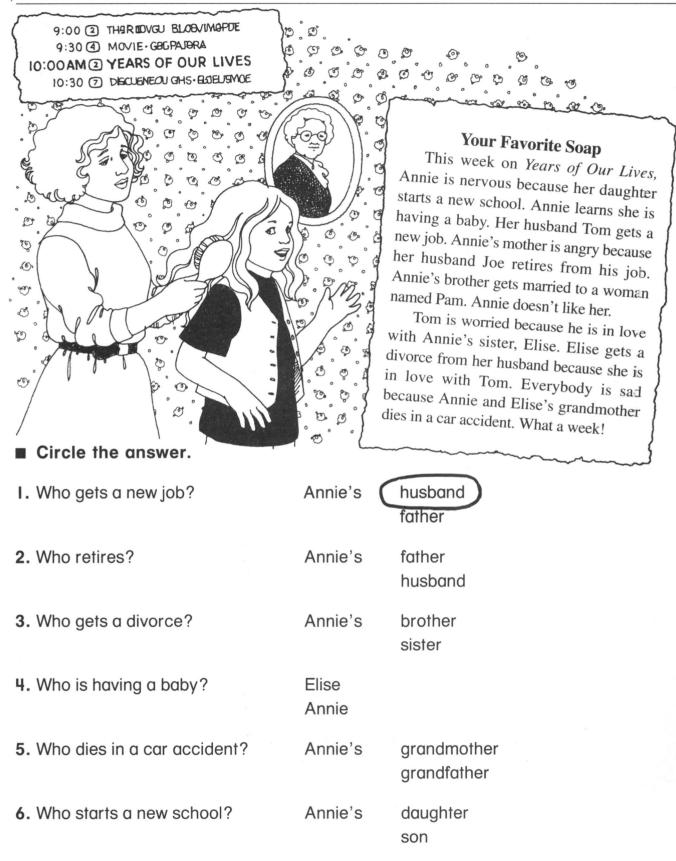

9:00 ② THE RADVGU BLOBVIMOPDE
9:30 ④ MOVIE·GBGPAJBRA
10:00AM ② YEARS OF OUR LIVES
10:30 ⑦ DISCUBNEOU GHS·BLJELISIMOE

Your Favorite Soap

This week on *Years of Our Lives,* Annie is nervous because her daughter starts a new school. Annie learns she is having a baby. Her husband Tom gets a new job. Annie's mother is angry because her husband Joe retires from his job. Annie's brother gets married to a woman named Pam. Annie doesn't like her.

Tom is worried because he is in love with Annie's sister, Elise. Elise gets a divorce from her husband because she is in love with Tom. Everybody is sad because Annie and Elise's grandmother dies in a car accident. What a week!

■ **Circle the answer.**

1. Who gets a new job?   Annie's   (husband)
                                           father

2. Who retires?   Annie's   father
                                           husband

3. Who gets a divorce?   Annie's   brother
                                           sister

4. Who is having a baby?   Elise
                                Annie

5. Who dies in a car accident? Annie's   grandmother
                                           grandfather

6. Who starts a new school?   Annie's   daughter
                                           son

4 Activity Sheets for The Home

* tapescript on p. 62

▪ A Good Excuse

Focused Listening I / Dictionary, p. 31
(No Activity Sheet)

Look at page 31 in your dictionary. Listen to Alex and Pearl. They are neighbors. Point to the pictures you hear them talking about.

Pearl: Hi! Alex. What's up? You don't look very happy.

Alex: Oh, Pearl, I feel terrible. A big branch from my tree fell on my roof and now my roof is leaking. I have broken steps that go up to my front porch and my toilet is stopped up. Oh, and the yard in the back is a mess.

Pearl: Alex, come here. Calm down. Here. You can borrow my **hammer** to fix the roof.*

Alex: Gee, thanks, but I don't really want...

Pearl: How about the **saw**? You can cut the branch in half with the saw.

Alex: A saw? Well, maybe, but...*

Pearl: And **nails**. I'm sure you need some nails. Take these. And the **flashlight** to see where the leaks are.

Alex: A flashlight? Listen, Pearl, I didn't come for that....*

Pearl: Now, let's see. For the broken steps you'll need some **screws**, and a **screwdriver**.

Alex: A screwdriver?

Pearl: I have an electric **drill**. Do you want that?

Alex: No, I really don't need a drill.*

Pearl: What else? For the toilet you'll need a **wrench**. Here, this wrench is new. Oh, and the **pliers**. Take the pliers, you never know.

Alex: Pearl, please...*

Pearl: Don't be silly. Here, take the **rake** to clean up the yard. And the **lawn mower**. Take the lawn mower to cut the grass. The **hose**... Do you need a hose?

Alex: Pearl, I don't want any of these things!

Pearl: You don't? Why not?

Alex: I just needed a good excuse to see you. Do you think we could go out sometime?

▪ Cleaning Crew

Focused Listening II / Activity Sheet, p. 63

Listen to the manager of a cleaning crew tell his workers what to do. Follow the directions on your paper.

1. All right everybody, we have 30 minutes before the party and a really dirty house. Let's get to work. Saul, you go into the **kitchen** and **dry the dishes** on the counter. They're clean, just dry them and put them away.

2. Felicia, please **sweep** the **halls**. The broom is in the closet. Don't forget to sweep under the stairs.

3. Raffi, you go upstairs to the **bedrooms** and **make all the beds**. Don't take off the sheets and blankets, just make the beds. Quickly, okay?

4. Terry, I want you to go upstairs with Raffi and **clean** the **bathrooms**. Don't worry about the toilets for now. Just clean up around the sinks.

5. Wally, take this bag and **empty the wastebasket** in the **living room**. Just leave the bag by the door. I can take it out later. Be sure to get all the papers that fell on the floor.

6. Margo, I need you to work outside. Can you **rake all the leaves** in the **backyard**? I think the rake is next to the lawn mower. (Pause) Me? What about me? I'm going to supervise. Come on, everybody, let's go!

▪ Where Does It Go?

Focused Listening II / Activity Sheet, p. 64

Listen to Mr. and Mrs. Goodman putting away the last few things in their home. Follow the directions on your paper.

1. Darling, just look at our lovely new home. And we only have a few things left to put away! Let's put that **hamper** in the bedroom, next to the **dresser**.

2. Of course, pumpkin, whatever you say. And let's put the **wastebasket** in the bedroom too, next to your side of the **bed**.

3. What a good idea, sugar plum! Don't you think we need to put the **lamp** near the bed. Let's put it on the **night table** next to your side of the bed.

4. Oh, sweet potato, the lamp looks wonderful. I just know the **rug** will look beautiful on the **floor** in front of the bed. Oh, I was right...

5. The rug is sensational, angel. What do you think about the **television**? On the **dresser**, maybe? That way we can watch TV in bed.

6. The TV fits perfectly, oh light-of-my-life. But what about this **table**? I know! I know! Under the **window**. Let's put it under the window... Ooh! It's just right.

Focused Listening II/Teacher's Notes, p. 3/Dictionary, pp. 22–30

■ **Fold your paper on the dotted line.**
■ **Listen and circle the letter under the correct picture.**

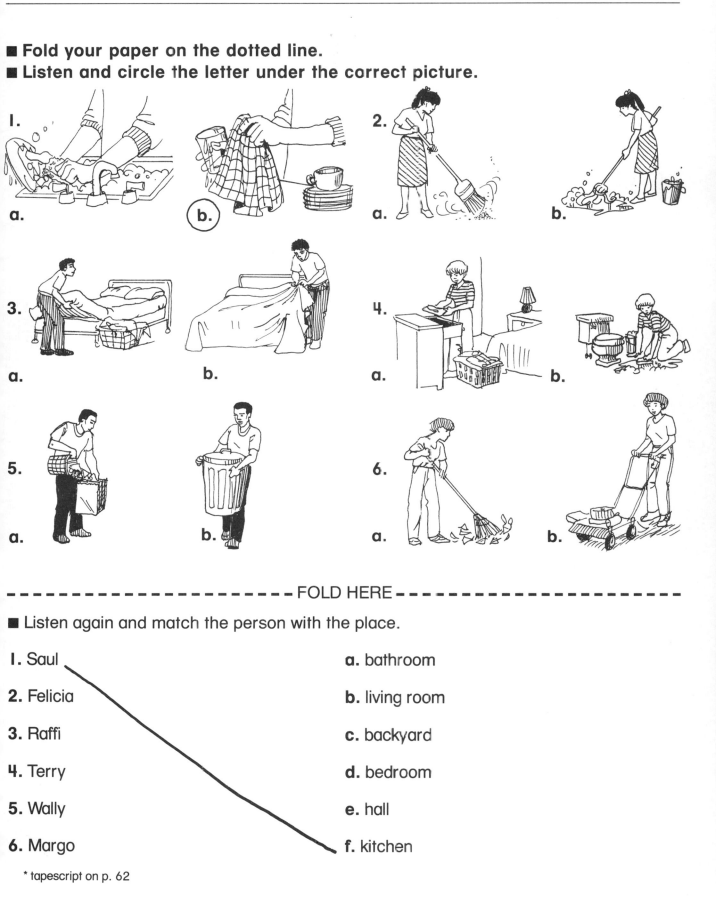

1.   a.   b.

2.   a.   b.

3.   a.   b.

4.   a.   b.

5.   a.   b.

6.   a.   b.

------------------------- FOLD HERE -------------------------

■ Listen again and match the person with the place.

1. Saul	**a.** bathroom
2. Felicia	**b.** living room
3. Raffi	**c.** backyard
4. Terry	**d.** bedroom
5. Wally	**e.** hall
6. Margo	**f.** kitchen

* tapescript on p. 62

Where Does It Go?*

Focused Listening II/Teacher's Notes, p. 3/Dictionary, pp. 24, 26–27

■ **Listen to Mr. and Mrs. Goodman putting away the last few things in their new home.**

■ **Write the letter on the correct line in the picture.**

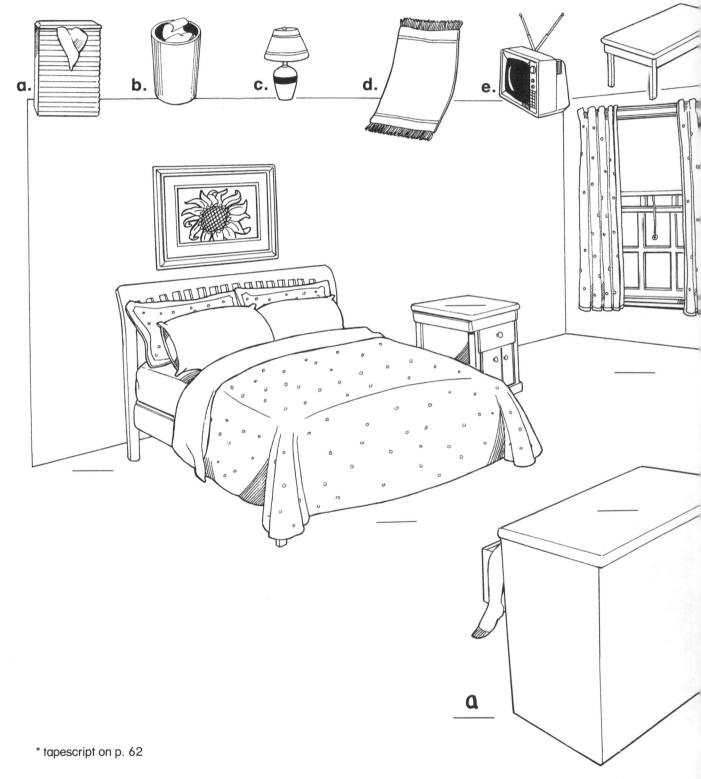

a.   b.   c.   d.   e.

a

* tapescript on p. 62

Washing Those Dirty Dishes

TPR Sequence/Teacher's notes, p. 4/Dictionary, pp. 28–29

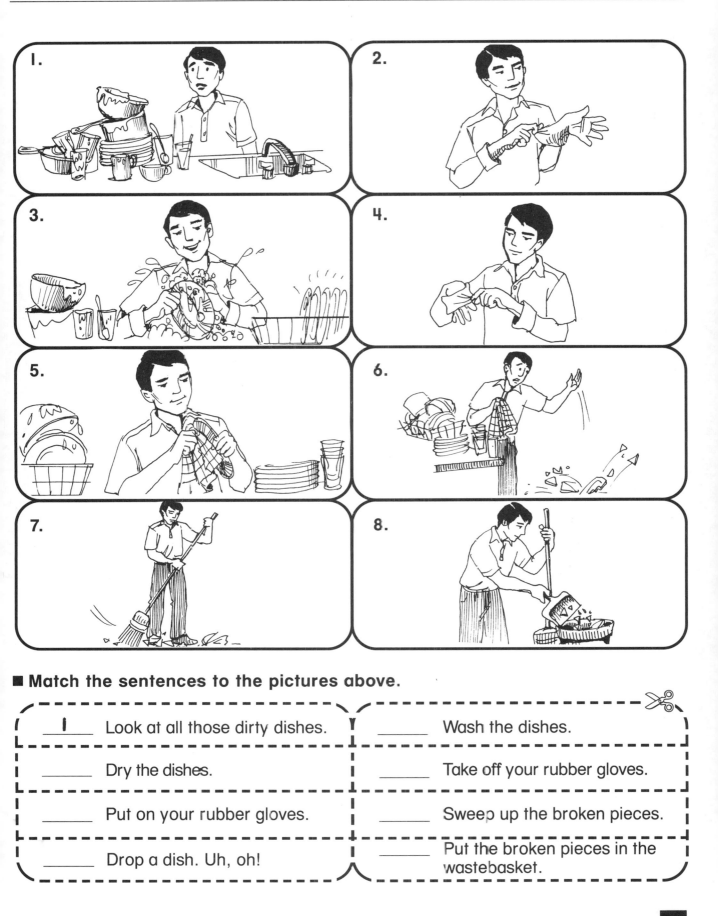

■ Match the sentences to the pictures above.

_1_	Look at all those dirty dishes.	_____	Wash the dishes.
_____	Dry the dishes.	_____	Take off your rubber gloves.
_____	Put on your rubber gloves.	_____	Sweep up the broken pieces.
_____	Drop a dish. Uh, oh!	_____	Put the broken pieces in the wastebasket.

A

1. ■ **Sit with a partner. Don't look at your partner's paper.**
   ■ **Look at the sign.**
   ■ **Answer your partner's questions.**

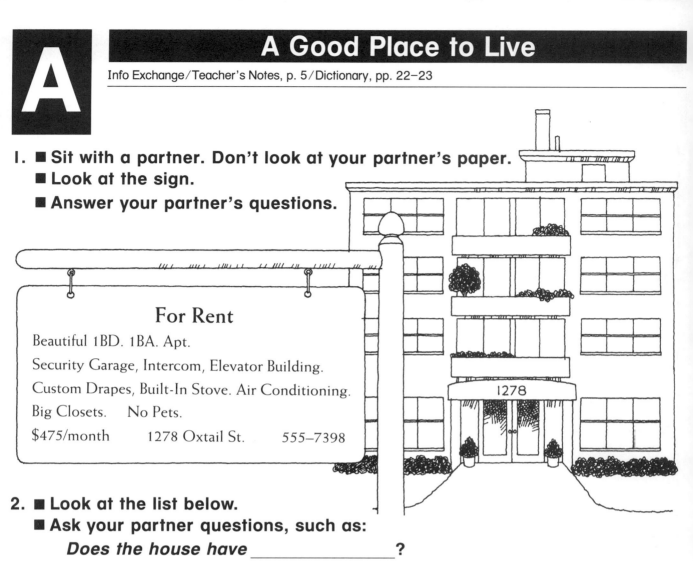

For Rent

Beautiful 1BD. 1BA. Apt.

Security Garage, Intercom, Elevator Building.

Custom Drapes, Built-In Stove. Air Conditioning.

Big Closets.   No Pets.

$475/month   1278 Oxtail St.   555–7398

2. ■ **Look at the list below.**
   ■ **Ask your partner questions, such as:**
       Does the house have _____?
   ■ **Mark the answers.**

		Yes	No
	a garage		
○	a backyard		
	a stove		
	a refrigerator		
	air conditioning		
	a patio		
	a garden		
○	a laundry room		

1. ■ **Sit with a partner. Don't look at your partner's paper.**
   ■ **Look at the list below.**
   ■ **Ask your partner questions, such as:**
   Does the apartment have _____?
   ■ **Mark the answers.**

	Yes	No
a garage		
an intercom		
a stove		
a refrigerator		
air conditioning		
a balcony		
drapes		
an elevator		

2. ■ **Look at the sign.**
   ■ **Answer your partner's questions.**

For Rent

Beautiful 3BD. 2BA. House, Big Garage
Brand New Refrigerator, Big Backyard
with Pool and Patio.
Big Closets, Cable TV. Pets, OK.
$700/month   1392 Palm Ave.   555–9378

Do You Do the Housework?

Interview/Teacher's Notes, p. 7/Dictionary, pp. 28–29

- **Read the questions and write your answers.**
- **Ask and answer the questions with your partner.**
- **Write your partner's answers.**

	My Answers	My Partner's Answers
1. Do you do the housework?		
2. Do you do the laundry?		
3. Do you fix things at home?		
4. Do you have electrical tools?		

- **Circle the correct words.**

You

1. I do / don't do the housework.
2. I do / don't do the laundry.
3. I fix / don't fix things at home.
4. I have / don't have electrical tools.

Your partner

1. He / She does / doesn't do the housework.
2. He / She does / doesn't do the laundry.
3. He / She fixes / doesn't fix things at home.
4. He / She has / doesn't have electrical tools.

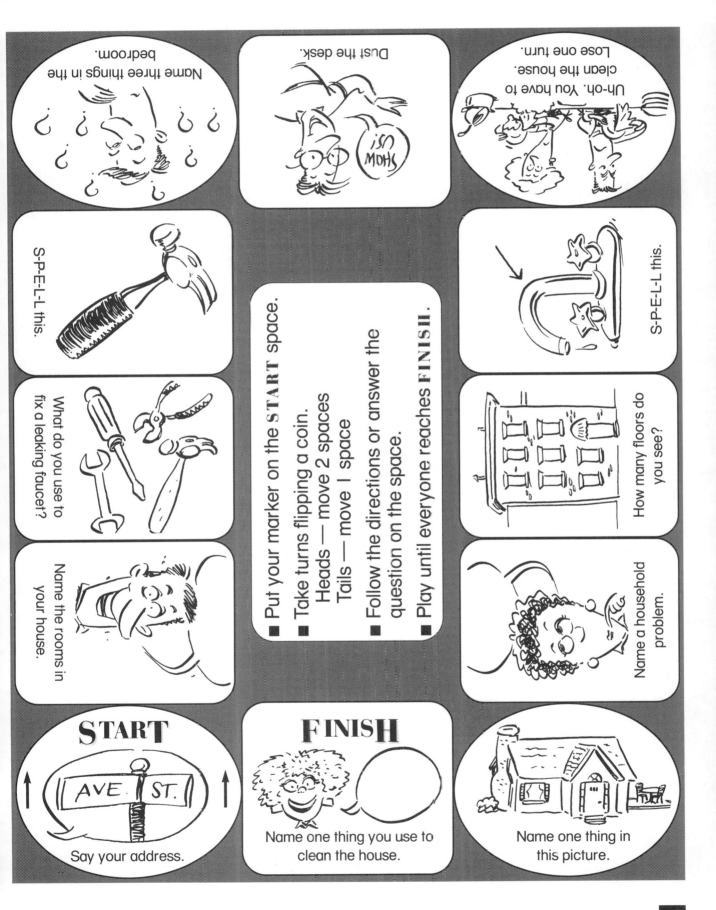

Name three things in the bedroom.

Dust the desk.

Uh-oh. You have to clean the house. Lose one turn.

S-P-E-L-L this.

S-P-E-L-L this.

What do you use to fix a leaking faucet?

How many floors do you see?

Name the rooms in your house.

Name a household problem.

- Put your marker on the START space.
- Take turns flipping a coin.
  Heads — move 2 spaces
  Tails — move 1 space
- Follow the directions or answer the question on the space.
- Play until everyone reaches FINISH.

START

AVE. ST.

Say your address.

FINISH

Name one thing you use to clean the house.

Name one thing in this picture.

■ **Look at the picture below.**
■ **Describe the problems in the apartment.**

■ **Copy the description.**

_____

_____

_____

_____

_____

_____

_____

Life Skills Reading/Teacher's Notes, p. 11/Dictionary, pp. 23–27

■ **Read the directory.**
■ **Circle these words:**

| alarm clocks | armchairs | drapes | stereos | towels |

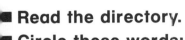

STORE DIRECTORY

1st Floor	**HOUSEWARES** Small Appliances • Dishes • Pots and Pans • Dish Towels • Kitchen Tools
	LIVING ROOM FURNISHINGS Sofas • Armchairs • End Tables • Coffee Tables
2nd Floor	**LARGE APPLIANCES** Washers • Dryers • Air Conditioners • Dishwashers • Stoves
	BED AND BATH Bedspreads • Blankets • Sheets • Drapes • Towels • Shower Curtains
3rd Floor	**ELECTRONICS** TVs • Stereos • Computers • Radios • Alarm Clocks

■ **Write the missing words.**

1. Dish towels are on the _____ 1st _____ floor.

2. The alarm clocks are near the radios
   on the _____ floor.

3. You can find drapes in Bed and Bath
   on the _____ floor.

4. Take the elevator to the _____ floor for stereos.

5. The armchairs are on the _____ floor near the
   entrance.

Forgetful Teresa

Narrative Reading/Teacher's Notes, p. 12/Dictionary, pp. 23–27

Teresa Richly lives in a large, expensive apartment. It has everything. In the living room there is a big, comfortable armchair for Teresa. In the bedroom there is a fabulous bed with a pretty bedspread. There is a telephone in every room in the apartment. There is a television in the bathroom and a stereo in the bedroom and the living room. But Teresa is not happy. Teresa is in the hall because she doesn't have her key. The key is in Teresa's kitchen.

■ **Circle the answer.**

1. Teresa lives in a large   (apartment.)
     house.

2. In every room there is a   television.
     telephone.

3. In the living room there is a comfortable   bed.
     chair.

4. Teresa doesn't have her   key.
     alarm clock.

5. Teresa is in the   kitchen.
     hall.

5 Activity Sheets for The Market

* tapescript on p. 74

■ Meat Cutting 101
Focused Listening I / Dictionary, p. 36
(No Activity Sheet)

Look at page 36 in your dictionary. Listen to the butcher teach the students about the different kinds of meat and seafood. Point to the items you hear him talking about.

Okay, future butchers, let's see what we have today. We're going to study **pork** cuts in this class. They're very popular and have to be just right. Here's a great **ham**. We'll practice cutting these little beauties next week.* I don't know how you like to start your morning, but I never forget the **bacon**. I like to cut a few slices of bacon every day.* Now if you want to see something really beautiful, just look at this **steak**. You'll have to cut a steak like this at the end of class.* Now if ya' don't cut the steak right, you have to put it in the grinder for **ground meat**. Ground meat covers up any mistake you make.* Next month you'll all have to practice on **lamb**. I love **lamb chops**, don't you?* Look over here. I brought in some poultry. This will be the last part of our course. You'll learn how to pluck and prepare **turkeys**, just in time for the holidays.* Now this class doesn't cover **seafood**, but I brought some for you to see anyway. You should all learn how to clean **fish**. Fish is really popular these days.* Oh, and don't be scared away from **shellfish**, like **lobster**. You can put these guys in a tank in your butcher shop and attract a lot of customers. So now you know all about the class. Anybody hungry?

■ Shopping List
Focused Listening II / Activity Sheet, p. 75

Listen to a husband and wife talk about what they need at the market. Follow the directions on your paper.

1. I think we need some things at the market. We're out of **yogurt**... and I think we need some **milk** too.

2. Oh, and I noticed we don't have any more **coffee**. We'd better pick up two jars.

3. Let's get some **cream** for a change. I really like cream in my coffee. I don't think we need sugar though.

4. I know the kids probably need some drinks. I'll pick up some apple **juice**. They love to take apple juice to school.

5. While you're at it, will you get me some **soda**? I don't see any in the refrigerator.

6. I think we need to get some **beans**, but we don't want any more noodles. We have 3 boxes of spaghetti in the cabinet.

7. I want to make **chicken** and rice for dinner tonight. Let's get a couple of pounds of chicken, but we don't need any rice. Get me some **onions**, too.

8. Let's get **strawberries** for the kids' dessert... ...and some **cookies** for us.

■ Putting the Groceries Away
Focused Listening II / Activity Sheet, p. 76

Listen to Mei Ying tell her granddaughter where to put the groceries. Follow the directions on your paper.

1. The **mayonnaise** goes **in the refrigerator**, **in the door**.

2. Please put the **grapes on the counter**, **in the bowl**.

3. Could you put the **tomatoes in the sink**? Put them **on the left side**. I want to wash them for our salad.

4. Put the **fish in the freezer**, **on the top shelf**. I can cook it on the weekend.

5. What's this? Oh, the **soap**. Let's put that **in the big drawer next to the dishwasher**.

6. Don't forget to put the cans of **soup in the cabinet**. Put them **on the second shelf**, okay? The first shelf is for cereal boxes.

Shopping List*

Focused Listening II/Teacher's Notes, p. 3/Dictionary, pp. 34–39

- **Fold your paper on the dotted line.**
- **Listen to a husband and wife talk about what they need at the market.**
- **Make a check (✔) next to the foods on their shopping list.**

Dairy	**Meat/Poultry**	**Fruit**	**Groceries**
✔ milk	___ ground meat	___ apples	___ sugar
___ cream	___ steak	___ bananas	___ flour
___ cheese	___ lamb	___ lemons	___ cereal
✔ yogurt	___ chicken	___ strawberries	___ salt
___ butter	___ pork ribs	___ watermelon	___ pepper
Bakery	**Rice/Pasta**	**Vegetables**	___ oil
___ cookies	___ beans	___ broccoli	___ coffee
___ bread	___ spaghetti	___ carrots	___ tea
___ cake	___ white rice	___ lettuce	___ soda
___ pie	___ brown rice	___ onions	___ juice

- - - - - - - - - - - - - - FOLD HERE - - - - - - - - - - - - - - - - -

- **Listen again and write the shopping list on the lines below.**
  Unfold the paper and check your spelling.

Shopping list	
yogurt, milk	

* tapescript on p. 74

Putting the Groceries Away*

Focused Listening II/Teacher's Notes, p. 3/Dictionary, pp. 25, 34–39

■ **Fold the paper on the dotted line.**

■ **Listen to Mei Ying tell her granddaughter where to put the groceries.**

■ **Match the food to the location.**

1. mayonnaise   _____ **a.** counter

2. grapes   _____ **b.** sink

3. tomatoes   ___1___ **c.** refrigerator

4. fish   _____ **d.** cabinet

5. soap   _____ **e.** drawer

6. soup   _____ **f.** freezer

- - - - - - - - - - - - - - - - - - - FOLD HERE - - - - - - - - - - - - - - - - - - -

■ **Listen again and write the number of each item in the correct location.**

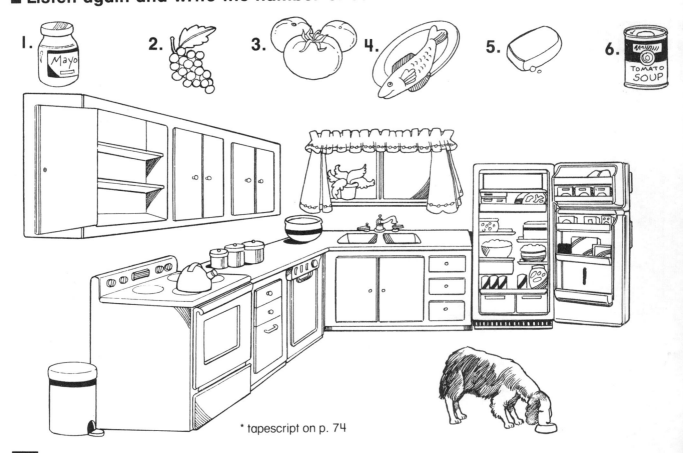

* tapescript on p. 74

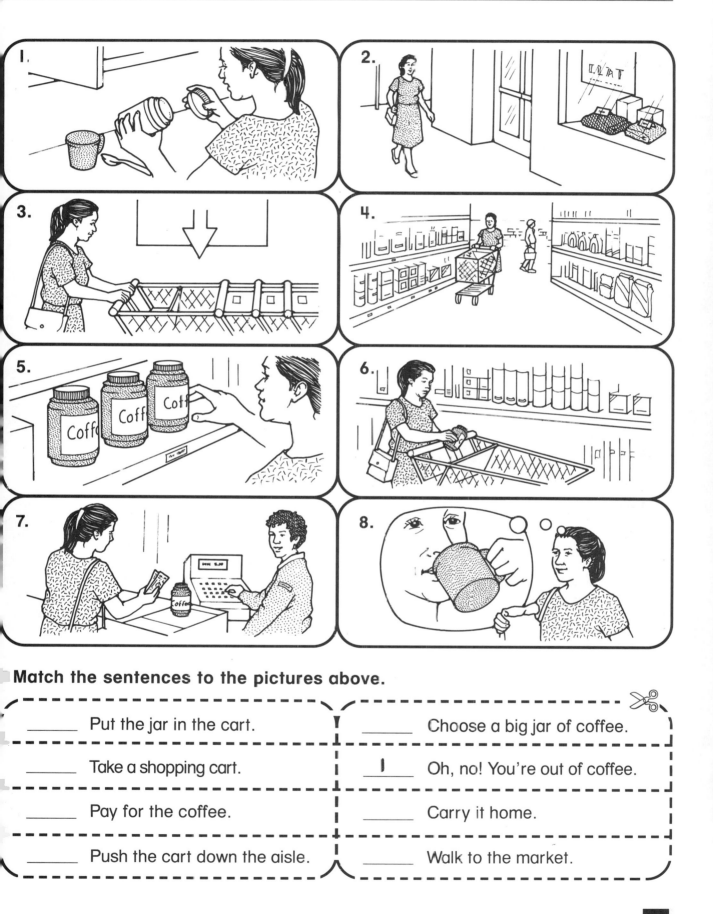

Match the sentences to the pictures above.

_____ Put the jar in the cart.

_____ Take a shopping cart.

_____ Pay for the coffee.

_____ Push the cart down the aisle.

_____ Choose a big jar of coffee.

___1___ Oh, no! You're out of coffee.

_____ Carry it home.

_____ Walk to the market.

1. Sit with a partner. Don't look at your partner's paper.
   You and your partner are going to make *Cold Day Vegetable Soup*.
   Read the recipe. Tell your partner what you need to buy.
   Spell any words your partner doesn't know.

> ### COLD DAY VEGETABLE SOUP
>
> Ingredients:
>
> | | |
> |---|---|
> | 1 box of rice | 2 carrots |
> | 2 onions | celery |
> | 3 potatoes | salt and pepper |
>
> Put all ingredients in a pot and cover with water.
> Cook for one hour. Serves 6.

2. You and your partner are going to make *Sunny Day Fruit Salad*.
   Listen to your partner read the recipe.
   Make a shopping list of the foods you need to buy.
   Ask your partner to spell any words you don't know.

1. ☐ Sit with a partner. Don't look at your partner's paper.
☐ You and your partner are going to make *Cold Day Vegetable Soup*.
☐ Listen to your partner read the recipe.
☐ Make a list of the foods you need to buy.
☐ Ask your partner to spell any words you don't know.

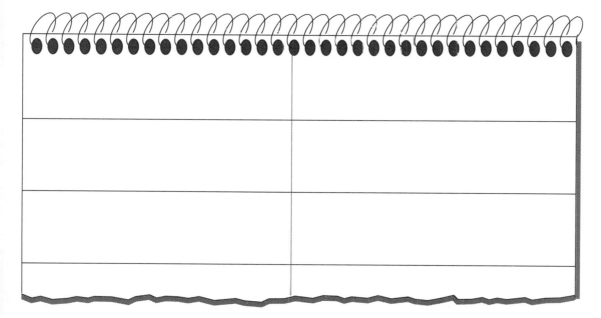

2. ☐ You and your partner are going to make *Sunny Day Fruit Salad*.
☐ Read the recipe. Tell your partner what you need to buy.
☐ Spell any words your partner doesn't know.

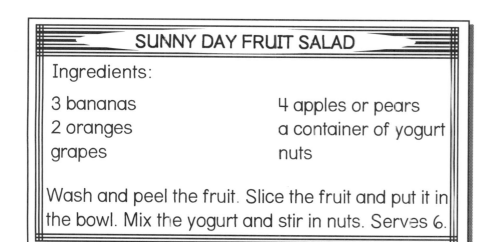

SUNNY DAY FRUIT SALAD

Ingredients:

3 bananas	4 apples or pears
2 oranges	a container of yogurt
grapes	nuts

Wash and peel the fruit. Slice the fruit and put it in the bowl. Mix the yogurt and stir in nuts. Serves 6.

What's in Your Kitchen?

Mixer/Teacher's Notes, p. 6/Dictionary, pp. 37–39

- ■ **Write the missing words.**
- ■ **Walk around the room. Ask and answer this question:**

  Do you have a _____ in your kitchen?
- ■ **Write a different name in each box.**

c a r t o n of milk	p _ c k _ g _ of cookies	b _ g of flour
b _ x of cereal	c _ n of soup	l _ _ f of bread
b _ t t l _ of soda	c _ n t _ _ n _ r of yogurt	j _ r of coffee

Board Game/Teacher's Notes, p. 8/Dictionary, pp. 34–40

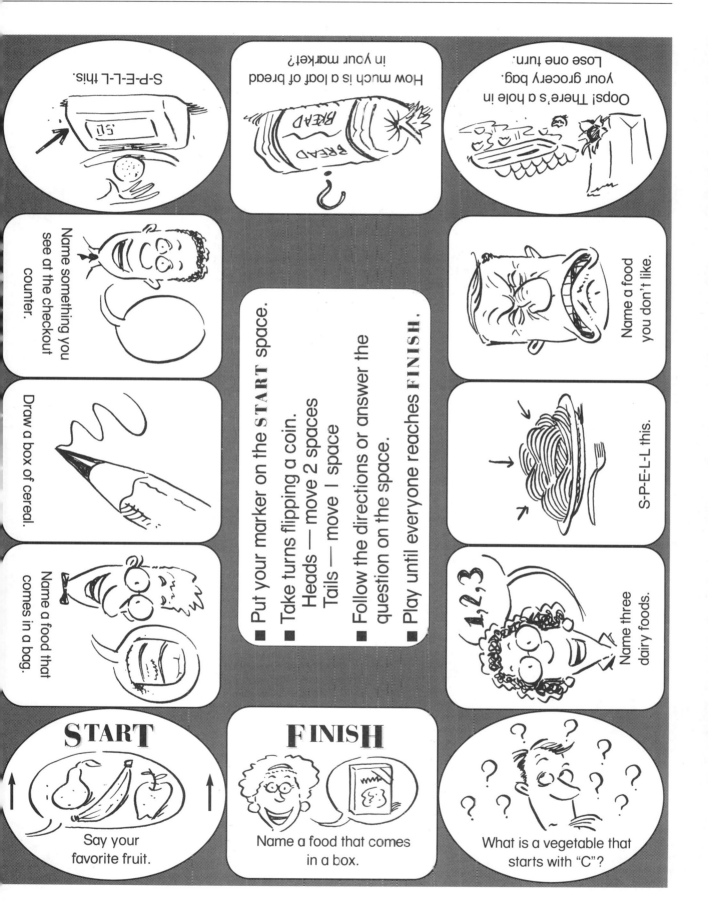

S-P-E-L-L this.

How much is a loaf of bread in your market?

Oops! There's a hole in your grocery bag. Lose one turn.

Name something you see at the checkout counter.

Name a food you don't like.

Draw a box of cereal.

S-P-E-L-L this.

- Put your marker on the **START** space.
- Take turns flipping a coin.
  Heads — move 2 spaces
  Tails — move 1 space
- Follow the directions or answer the question on the space.
- Play until everyone reaches **FINISH**.

Name a food that comes in a bag.

Name three dairy foods.

START
Say your favorite fruit.

FINISH
Name a food that comes in a box.

What is a vegetable that starts with "C"?

LEA Project/Teacher's Notes, p. 10/Dictionary, pp. 34–39

THE PROJECT

■ **You are going to make sandwiches with your classmates.
Then you will talk, write, and read about the experience.**

■ **Your teacher is going to put the <u>sandwich ingredients</u> on a big table.**

DIRECTIONS

1. Get <u>paper plates</u>, a <u>plastic knife</u>,
   and <u>two slices of bread</u> from your teacher.

2. Choose two food items from the main table
   and take them to your desk.

3. Make your sandwich and cut it in half.
   Put it on the plate.

4. Offer half your sandwich to a classmate.
   Try a classmate's sandwich.

5. Describe the experience to your teacher.
   (Your teacher will write what you say on the board.)

6. Look at the sentences on the board and copy them.

7. Read the sentences to a classmate.

Food Labels

■ **Read the information on the labels.**
■ **Circle these words:**

> **ingredients   oil   salt   sugar   water**

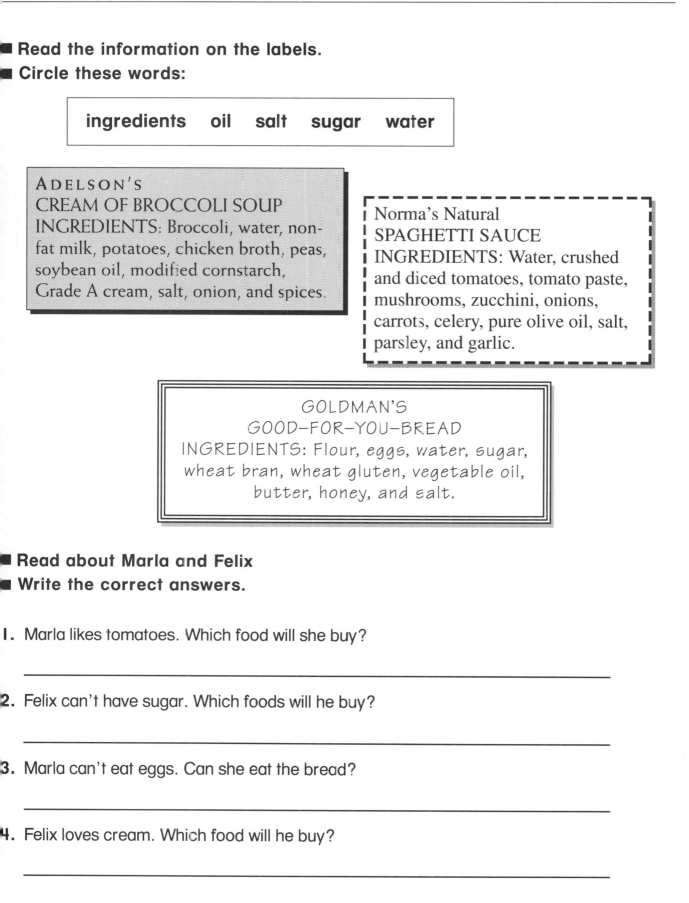

ADELSON'S
CREAM OF BROCCOLI SOUP
INGREDIENTS: Broccoli, water, non-fat milk, potatoes, chicken broth, peas, soybean oil, modified cornstarch, Grade A cream, salt, onion, and spices.

Norma's Natural
SPAGHETTI SAUCE
INGREDIENTS: Water, crushed and diced tomatoes, tomato paste, mushrooms, zucchini, onions, carrots, celery, pure olive oil, salt, parsley, and garlic.

GOLDMAN'S
GOOD—FOR—YOU—BREAD
INGREDIENTS: Flour, eggs, water, sugar, wheat bran, wheat gluten, vegetable oil, butter, honey, and salt.

■ **Read about Marla and Felix**
■ **Write the correct answers.**

1. Marla likes tomatoes. Which food will she buy?

_____

2. Felix can't have sugar. Which foods will he buy?

_____

3. Marla can't eat eggs. Can she eat the bread?

_____

4. Felix loves cream. Which food will he buy?

_____

I'm Saul Bernstein. I work at *Shopping Basket Market*. It's a nice, small market and I have many jobs. Sometimes I'm the stockboy. I put packages, boxes, and cans on the shelves. Sometimes I'm the bagger. I put the groceries in the bags and carry them for the customers. Sometimes I'm the janitor. I sweep the floors and wash the windows. On Tuesday afternoons I work at the bottle return. I count the bottles. On Saturdays I work at the checkout counter. I like to work with the cash register.

Shopping Basket Market is a wonderful place to work. It's great to have a different job every day.

■ **Match the sentences.**

1. Saul puts packages on the shelf.   ____ **a.** He's a clerk.

2. Saul puts the groceries in the bag.   ____ **b.** He's a janitor.

3. Saul buys groceries.   _1_ **c.** He's a stockboy.

4. Saul uses the cash register.   ____ **d.** He's a customer.

5. Saul sweeps the floor.   ____ **e.** He's a bagger.

6 Activity Sheets for Meal Time

* tapescript on p. 86

Unit 6 Meal Time Tapescripts

Family Dinner

Focused Listening I / Dictionary, p. 42
(No Activity Sheet)

Look at page 42 in your dictionary. Listen to Mrs. Green talk about her family as they set the table. Point to the people and things you hear her talking about.

Mrs. Green: Just look at my family, all helping set the table for dinner. They're such good kids. That's Pat, my oldest boy. He's putting plates on the table. He's put two down, and he's on the third **plate**. Pat, set only four places tonight, Dad has to work late.* That's right, Robin, the **fork** goes on the left. (Robin, my youngest, is just learning how to set the table. He's watching his brother, and getting help.)* Where's the rest of the **silverware**? Oh, it's over there, I see it at the other side of the table.* Don't forget to put out the **knife** and **spoon** like Pat did over there. The knife goes next to the plate, on the right, and the spoon goes next to the knife.* Toni knows how to fold a **napkin** ten different ways. Tonight I see she's folded the napkins into triangles. Toni, I like the way you put them on the **placemat**.* I'm the only one who gets a **cup** and **saucer** tonight .We'll put the ones on the counter away.* Did you put the glasses out? We each get a **glass** of water tonight.* Move the **salt and pepper shakers** into the center of the table. I'm not sure, but I think this chili I'm cooking might need a little salt.* Robin, bring me the **bowl**, please. I'm going take the fruit out and use the bowl for our salad.

M1:   Aw, mom!

M2:   Maw...

F1:   No!

Mrs. Green: Now, kids, come on. You know you need to eat more vegetables!

Are You Ready to Order?

Focused Listening II / Activity Sheet, p. 87

Listen to the waiter and his customers. Follow the directions on your paper.

1. Are you ready to order yet?

    I'll just have **coffee** and something sweet.

    We have donuts and muffins.

    I'll have a **donut**, please. A sugar donut.

2. And you ma'am?

    I'll have **pancakes** with lots of butter and maple syrup.

    Was that pancakes or waffles?

    Pancakes, please.

3. And you, sir?

    I'd like **scrambled eggs with sausage**, please.

    Did you say scrambled or fried?

Scrambled eggs, please. No toast.

4. What'll you have?

    I'm really hungry. I'm going to have some **fried chicken** and **mashed potatoes**.

    Was that baked or mashed potatoes?

    Mashed, please, with lots of gravy.

5. And you sir? What can I get for you?

    I'm not very hungry at all. How about an order of buttered toast?

    Would you like to try one of our English muffins?

    No, **toast**, with butter and jam.

6. Will there be anything else?

    I'd like some **tea**.

    And water for everyone, please.

    One tea and 5 glasses of water. Very good.

Cook It Right!

Focused Listening II / Activity Sheet, p. 88

Listen to Harry and Harriet explain how to cook healthy food. Follow the directions on your paper.

Good morning, everybody. This is "Cook It Right!" with Harry and Harriet. Today we're going to show you how to cook so your family stays healthy. You should eat lots of vegetables, with beans or fish, and not too much meat. And how you cook it is very important. Let's cook it rrright!

1. Harriet is **broiling** the fish. See how she puts it in under the **broiler** and **broils** it for just ten minutes, until it is done? That's healthy, and good for your heart.

2. And here's Harry **steaming** vegetables. He cut them up and put them in the **steamer**, and put the lid on tight. Now the **steam** is cooking the vegetables quickly and easily. Open it up, Harry. Look how green and healthy the **steamed** broccoli is.

3. Another way to cook your vegetables is to do what the Chinese do. Cut the veggies up into pieces, put a little oil in a heavy pan, and **fry** everything very quickly. Remember to **stir** all the time. We call this **stir-fry** and it's very healthy too. You can add small strips of meat and ginger, or scallions. Look at that **stir-fry**, with peppers, onions, and other vegetables. Doesn't it make you hungry?

4. Here's a way to cook eggs without fat! Put eggs in a pot of cold water and **boil** the water. You can make **hard boiled** or **soft boiled** eggs this way. Just change the amount of time you **boil** the eggs. When you **boil** eggs they're better for you. Just don't add too much salt!

5. Maybe you're saying,"But what makes me fat is all the cakes and cookies and **baked** goods I eat." So watch us next Tuesday and we'll show you how to **bake** healthy **baked** goods. Let's cook it rrright!

■ **Fold your paper on the dotted line.**
■ **Listen to the waiter and his customers.**
■ **Circle the foods the customers order.**

1.

2.

3.

4.

5.

6.

- FOLD HERE -

■ **Listen again to the waiter and his customers.**
■ **Check (✓) what each customer will use.**

	teaspoon	fork	knife	cup	glass	small plate	big plate
1.	✓			✓		✓	
2.							
3.							
4.							
5.							
6.							

* tapescript on p. 86

■ **Fold your paper on the dotted line.**
■ **Listen to Harry and Harriet tell how to cook healthy food.**
■ **Circle how to cook the different foods.**

1. grate   (broil)   boil

2. stir   peel   steam

3. stir-fry   peel   grate

4. slice   boil   broil

5. bake   chop   grate

- - - - - - - - - - - - - - - - - - - FOLD HERE - - - - - - - - - - - - - - - - - -

■ **Listen again to the tape and write the correct number under each picture.**

* tapescript on p. 86

A Guest for Dinner

TPR Sequence/Teacher's Notes, p. 4/Dictionary, pp. 42-46

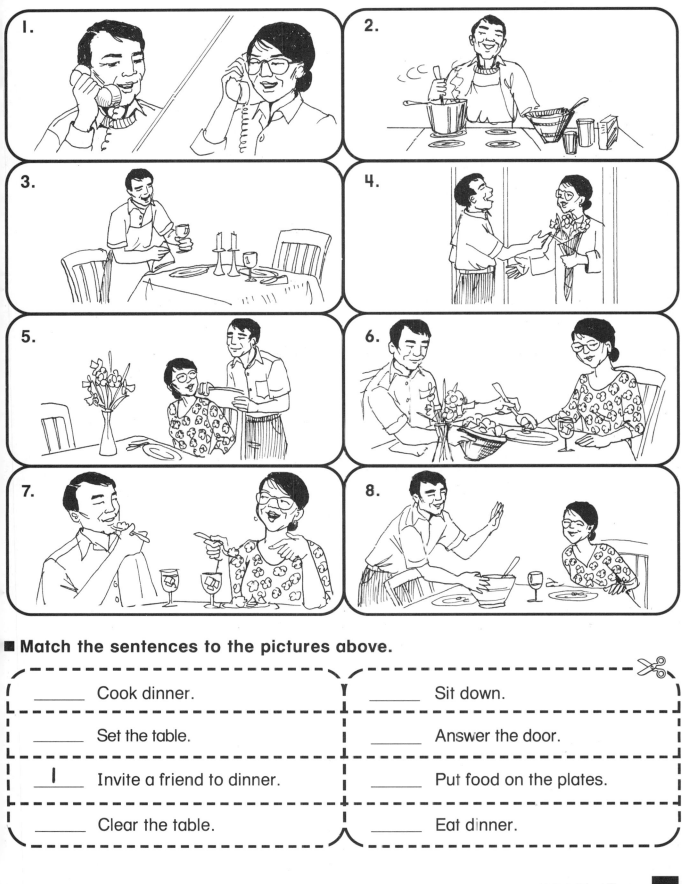

■ Match the sentences to the pictures above.

_____ Cook dinner.

_____ Sit down.

_____ Set the table.

_____ Answer the door.

__1__ Invite a friend to dinner.

_____ Put food on the plates.

_____ Clear the table.

_____ Eat dinner.

1. ■ **Sit with a partner. Don't look at your partner's paper.**
   ■ **Look at the menu.**
   ■ **Ask your partner for the missing prices:**
      How much is _____ *?*
   ■ **Write the prices on the menu.**

McWilliam's
Menu

Hamburger	$3.00
Hamburger with French Fries	_____
Hot Dog	1.50
Slice of Pizza	_____
Chicken Sandwich	_____
Green Salad	1.75
Ice Cream	1.25
Donut	_____
Pie	1.10
Soda	$1.00
Coffee	.75
Juice	1.25

2. ■ **Listen to your partner's questions.**
   ■ **Look at the menu and answer the questions.**

1. ■ **Sit with a partner. Don't look at your partner's paper.**
   ■ **Listen to your partner's questions.**
   ■ **Look at the menu and answer the questions.**

McWilliam's
Menu

Hamburger	$3.00
Hamburger with French Fries	4.50
Hot Dog	_____
Slice of Pizza	1.75
Chicken Sandwich	2.25
Green Salad	_____
Ice Cream	1.25
Donut	.90
Pie	_____
Soda	**$1.00**
Coffee	.75
Juice	_____

2. ■ **Ask your partner for the missing prices:**
   How much is_____?
   ■ **Write the prices on the menu.**

Do You Eat Pizza?

■ **Read the questions and write your answers.**
■ **Ask and answer the questions with your partner.**
■ **Write your partner's answers.**

	My Answers	My Partner's Answers
1. Do you eat pizza?		
2. Do you like hot dogs?		
3. Do you cook spaghetti?		
4. Do you fry eggs?		
5. Do you eat at restaurants?		

■ **Circle the correct words.**

You

1. I   eat / don't eat   pizza.

2. I   like / don't like   hot dogs.

3. I   cook / don't cook   spaghetti.

4. I   fry / don't fry   eggs.

5. I   go / don't go   to restaurants.

Your partner

1. He / She   eats / doesn't eat   pizza.

2. He / She   likes / doesn't like   hot dogs.

3. He / She   cooks / doesn't cook   spaghetti.

4. He / She   fries / doesn't fry   eggs.

5. He / She   goes / doesn't go   to restaurants.

Meal Time

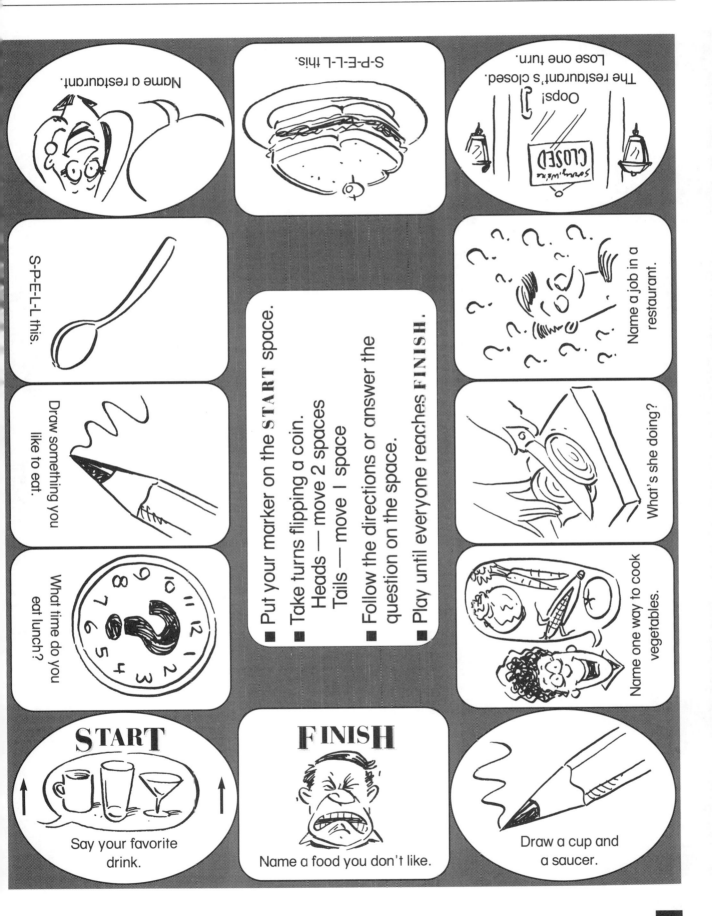

Name a restaurant.

S-P-E-L-L this.

Oops!
The restaurant's closed.
Lose one turn.

CLOSED

S-P-E-L-L this.

Name a job in a restaurant.

Draw something you like to eat.

- Put your marker on the START space.
- Take turns flipping a coin.
  Heads — move 2 spaces
  Tails — move 1 space
- Follow the directions or answer the question on the space.
- Play until everyone reaches FINISH.

What's she doing?

What time do you eat lunch?

Name one way to cook vegetables.

START
Say your favorite drink.

FINISH
Name a food you don't like.

Draw a cup and a saucer.

LEA Picture/Teacher's Notes, p. 9/Dictionary, p. 43

■ **Look at the picture.**
■ **Describe what's happening in the restaurant.**

■ **Copy the description.**

_____

_____

_____

_____

_____

_____

_____

A Recipe

Life Skills Reading/Teacher's Notes, p. 11/Dictionary, pp. 44–46 and Appendix

■ **Read the recipe.**

■ **Circle these words:** | cup   ingredients   tablespoon   teaspoon

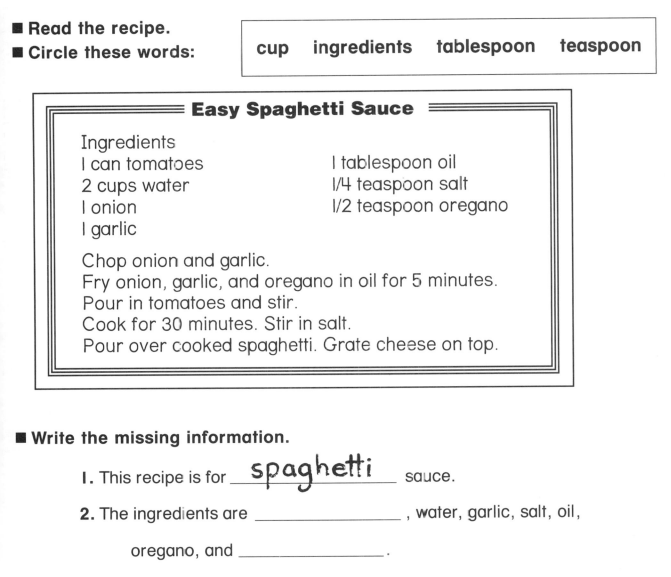

Easy Spaghetti Sauce

Ingredients
1 can tomatoes
2 cups water
1 onion
1 garlic

1 tablespoon oil
1/4 teaspoon salt
1/2 teaspoon oregano

Chop onion and garlic.
Fry onion, garlic, and oregano in oil for 5 minutes.
Pour in tomatoes and stir.
Cook for 30 minutes. Stir in salt.
Pour over cooked spaghetti. Grate cheese on top.

■ **Write the missing information.**

1. This recipe is for ___spaghetti___ sauce.

2. The ingredients are _____ , water, garlic, salt, oil,

   oregano, and _____ .

3. Chop and fry the onion and garlic in 1 _____ oil.

4. Pour in the _____ and _____ .

5. Cook for _____ minutes or _____ hour.

■ **Write the ingredients for something you like to cook.**

_____

_____

_____

I'm Ken and I'm single. I don't like to cook. Every morning I go
to a coffee shop and have pancakes. When the coffee cart comes at work,
I have a donut and more coffee.

At noon I eat a sandwich. On the way home I stop for a slice of pizza.
In the evening, at 8:00 p.m., I go to a restaurant and meet my friends.
I don't look at the menu. I always have chicken and french fries. At home
I watch TV and have some ice cream. I don't like to cook, but I always like to eat.

■ **Circle the answer.**

1. Ken eats pizza and ice cream for
   breakfast.
   lunch.
   (snacks.)

2. Ken eats a sandwich for
   breakfast.
   lunch.
   dinner.

3. Ken has a donut for
   coffee break.
   dinner.
   lunch.

4. Ken has chicken and french fries for
   dinner.
   snacks.
   breakfast.

5. Ken has pancakes for
   snacks.
   breakfast.
   dinner.

7 Activity Sheets for Clothing

* tapescript on p. 98

Unit 7 Clothing Tapescripts

■ Let's Go Shopping.
Focused Listening I/Dictionary, pp. 52–53
(No Activity Sheet)

Look at pages 52 and 53 in your dictionary. Listen to Barry and Donna talk about the clothes they need to buy for a wedding. Point to the clothes they're talking about.

Barry: Donna, we have to buy some new clothes for that wedding next week. But I'll just put on a T-shirt and jeans now. Ugh! This T-shirt is too **tight**! It's very uncomfortable. I don't like wearing tight T-shirts. Ah! This is better. A nice, big, **loose** T-shirt. That's more like it.

Donna: Barry, the radio said 50° to 60° today. I'm sure you're going to need a jacket when we go outside. Of course a **light** jacket's all you need in the mall. Fine. We're ready to go. Now, remember first we really have to go to the shoe store. I must get **high** heels. Everybody'll be wearing heels at the wedding.

Barry: And I have to get a **new** shirt! I think a blue shirt will go with my suit, won't it? All my shirts are **old** and most of them are **dirty**.

Donna: Of course you need a new shirt, you have to look good for the wedding. Come to think of it, I need to find a **long** skirt for the wedding. Long skirts are so elegant. Remind me to look at the long skirts.

Barry: Right. And you remind me to look for a tie. I don't have a tie. I want polka dot—I think. Certainly, polka dot goes with anything. But I want to get a **wide** tie. A wide, polka dot tie.

Donna: Okay, hop on the bike, baby, zip up that jacket and let's hit the stores!

■ A Day at the Beach
Focused Listening II/Activity Sheet, p. 99

Listen to Jill describe her friends at the beach. Follow the directions on your paper.

1. What a great day! Everyone is at the beach. Who's that in the **baseball cap**? Oh, it's Bill. Bill's wearing his Mets baseball cap.

2. Who's that with him in **shorts**? Is it Ann? Yes, it is Ann. She sure looks good in shorts.

3. And look, do you see Olga in her new striped **swimsuit**? Olga's a knockout in that bathing suit.

4. Oh, I see. She and Bob are going into the water for a swim. Bob's got his **swim trunks** on. Last week he had a new bathing suit on.

5. Hmmm. There's Myra on the boardwalk, too, wearing **jeans** and a **T-shirt**. She thinks it's sunny enough for sunglasses, but not for swimming. Hi, Myra.

6. Now Pat has the right idea! Here she comes, jogging by in her **warm-up suit**. Hi, Pat. Getting your exercise before you go in the water? Pat! Wait, I think I'll join you!

■ Stacy's Department Store
Focused Listening II/Activity Sheet, p. 100

Listen to the customers talk to the salesperson. Circle the items of clothing they want to find.

1. May I help you?

   Yes, please. Where are men's shoes?

   We carry a wide variety of **men's shoes** in the back of the store. Next to men's sleepwear.

2. What can I do for you?

   I'm looking for suits.

   Women's or men's?

   Women's, please.

   You can find **women's suits** across from dresses.

3. Can I be of service?

   Yes, thanks. I can't find **mittens** anywhere.

   Oh, they're with women's accessories, next to the jewelry counter.

   Women's accessories, next to the jewelry counter. Thanks.

4. Er, miss?

   Yes? How may I help you?

   Could you tell me where **sleepwear** is located?

   Certainly. It's next to women's shoes, near the stairs.

   Thank you.

5. Uh… ma'am… Can you help me?

   Of course. What can I do for you?

   Tell me where I can find **umbrellas**.

   Umbrellas are in men's sportswear.

   Thanks a lot.

6. Which way are the…

   Excuse me?

   The vests. I'm going camping. I need a **down vest**.

   Down vests and jackets are next to our camping equipment, in the far right corner of the store.

   Thank you.

A Day at the Beach *

- **Fold your paper on the dotted line.**
- **Listen to Jill describe her friends at the beach.**
- **Write the correct names on the lines.**

  1. Bill   *2. Ann*   *3. Olga*   *4. Bob*   *5. Myra*   *6. Pat*

Bill

- FOLD HERE -

- **Listen again. Match the names to the clothes.**

1. Bill	___ **a.** warm-up suit
2. Ann	___ **b.** swimsuit
3. Olga	___ **c.** jeans, T-shirt
4. Bob	_i_ **d.** baseball cap
5. Myra	___ **e.** swim trunks
6. Pat	___ **f.** shorts

* tapescript on p. 98

■ **Listen to the customers talk to the salesperson.**
■ **Circle the item of clothing they want to find.**

1.

2.

3.

4.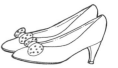

5.

6.

* tapescript on p. 98

I'll Do the Laundry

TPR Sequence/Teacher's Notes, p. 4/Dictionary, p. 56

Match the sentences to the pictures above.

_____ Fold the clothes.		_____ Pour detergent into the machine.	
_____ Start the machine.		_____ Unload the washing machine.	
_____ Dry the clothes.		___1___ Oh no! The laundry basket is full!	
_____ Iron some clothes.		_____ Load the washing machine.	

She Can't Find Her Shoes!

Info Exchange/Teacher's Notes, p. 5/Dictionary, pp. 48–55

1. ■ Sit with a partner. Don't look at your partner's paper.
   ■ Look at the picture below.
   ■ Tell your partner the location of these items:

   shoes   sunglasses   gloves   jeans   socks

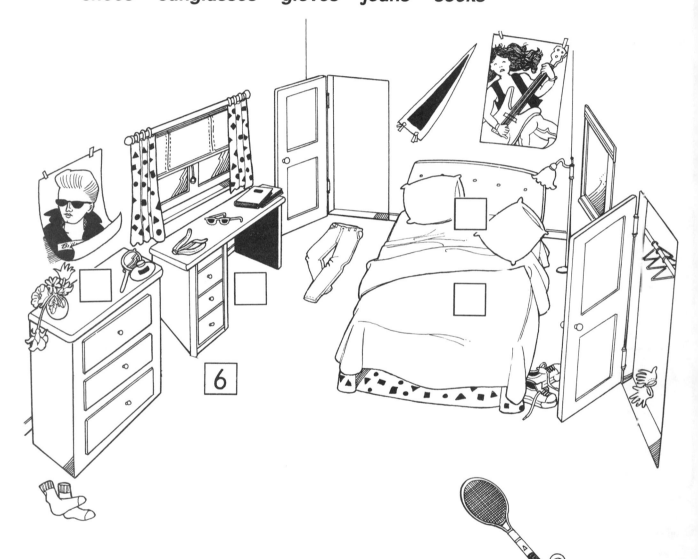

2. ■ Look at the picture and listen to your partner.
   ■ Write the numbers next to these items in the spaces:

   6. hat   7. backpack   8. ring   9. necklace   10. nightgown

1. ■ Sit with a partner. Don't look at your partner's paper.
■ Look at the picture below and listen to your partner.
■ Write the numbers next to these items in the spaces:
  1. shoes   2. sunglasses   3. gloves   4. jeans   5. socks

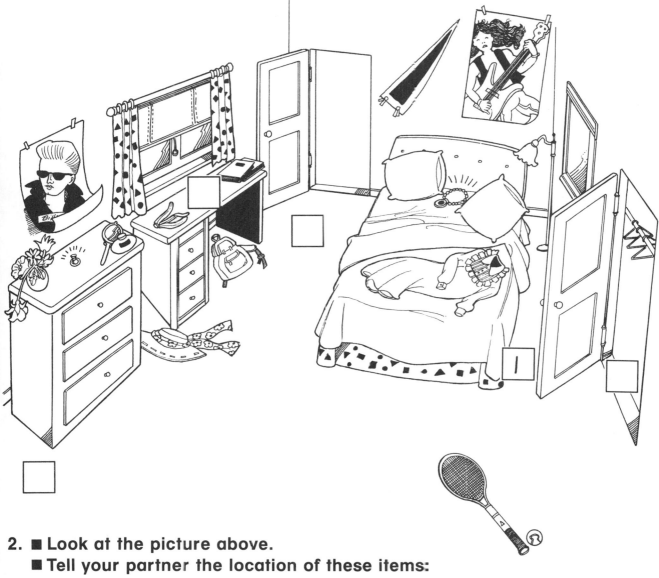

2. ■ Look at the picture above.
■ Tell your partner the location of these items:
  hat   backpack   ring   necklace   nightgown

■ **Walk around the room. Ask and answer this question:**

What size_____ do you wear?

■ **Write a different name on each line.**

■ **Write the size under the name.**

1. sneakers   Name _____

                   Size   _____

2. jeans   Name _____

                   Size   _____

3. T-shirt   Name _____

                   Size   _____

4. blouse   Name _____

                   Size   _____

5. socks   Name _____

                   Size   _____

6. dress   Name _____

                   Size   _____

7. shirt   Name _____

                   Size   _____

8. jacket   Name _____

                   Size   _____

Board Game/Teacher's Notes, p. 8/Dictionary, pp. 48–57

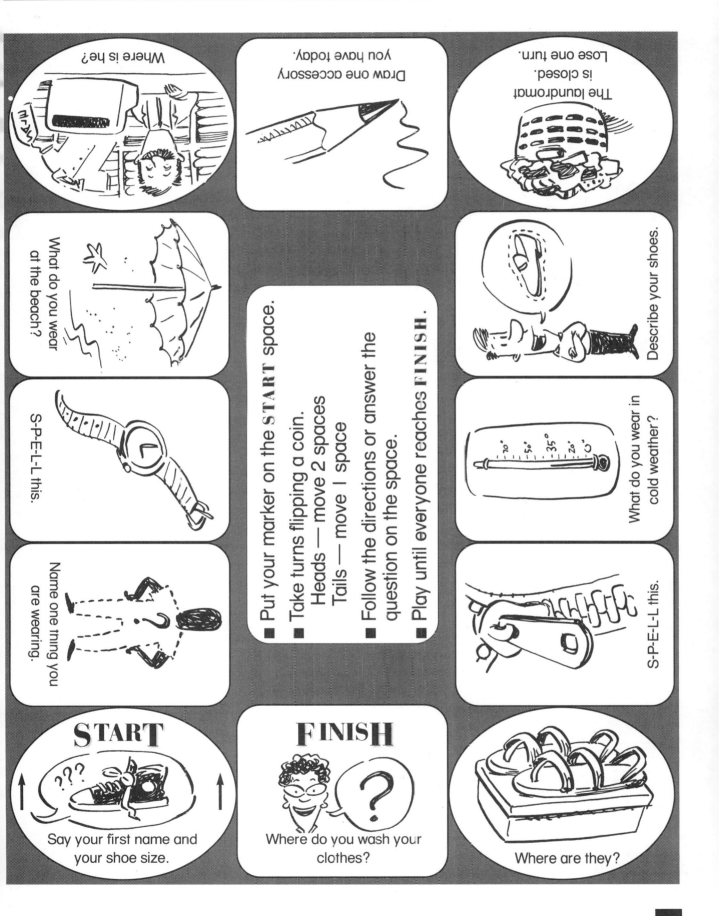

Where is he?

Draw one accessory you have today.

The laundromat is closed. Lose one turn.

What do you wear at the beach?

Describe your shoes.

S-P-E-L-L this.

- Put your marker on the **START** space.
- Take turns flipping a coin.
  Heads — move 2 spaces
  Tails — move 1 space
- Follow the directions or answer the question on the space.
- Play until everyone reaches **FINISH**.

What do you wear in cold weather?

Name one thing you are wearing.

S-P-E-L-L this.

START

Say your first name and your shoe size.

FINISH

Where do you wash your clothes?

Where are they?

Whoops! Wrong Dressing Room!

LEA Picture/Teacher's Notes, p. 9/Dictionary, pp. 48–57

■ **Look at the picture.**
■ **Describe the dressing room to your teacher.**

■ **Copy the description.**

_____

_____

_____

_____

_____

_____

_____

A Department Store Receipt

Life Skills Reading/Teacher's Notes, p. 11/Dictionary, pp. 48–55

■ **Read the receipt.**
■ **Circle these words:**

| cash | change | large | size | total | tax | XL |

```
          Dixon's Department Store
               24 Grand Street
          New Amsterdam, New York

123567    3 SHIRTS SIZE 17 AT 9.99        29.97
543210    3 PAIRS OF SOCKS, LARGE          7.00
987654    2 PAIRS XL WORK PANTS AT 29.99  58.98
789012    4 MEN'S BRIEF UNDERWEAR L       16.00
----------------------------------------------
 SUBTOTAL----------------------------->  111.95
 TAX----------------------------------->    8.85
 TOTAL--------------------------------->  120.80
 CASH                                     125.00
 CHANGE-------------------------------->    4.20
```

■ **Write the missing information.**

1. The customer wears size ____17____ shirts.

2. The customer wears size _____ pants.

3. One pair of work pants costs_____ .

4. The tax on the bill is _____ .

5. The total is_____ .

6. The customer paid with _____ and got _____ change.

Clothing a Family These Days

Narrative Reading/Teacher's Notes, p. 12/Dictionary, pp. 49–56

These days it's very expensive to buy clothing for a family. My children want special name-brand sneakers. Jack, my teenager, wants designer jeans or special sports shirts. Even the baby's clothes cost a lot and only fit for a few months.

My husband, Jim, needs new shirts for work, and I have to buy work clothes too. "Franny," my husband says, "sometimes I think we spend most of our money on clothes."

Yesterday a friend took me to the Third Street Thrift Shop. You can buy good clothes for less money there. The clothes are recycled. People give the store the clothes they can't use, and the thrift shop workers clean and iron the clothing. Now, I have a nice wool coat and it only cost $19.00! I can't wait to take my family!

■ Circle the answer.

1. Do Fran's children often ask for special clothes? (Yes) No

2. Does her husband need new sneakers? Yes No

3. Does Fran's family spend a lot of money on clothes? Yes No

4. Is the Third Street Thrift Shop an expensive store? Yes No

5. Did Fran buy a wool hat at the Thrift Shop? Yes No

6. Does she want to take her family to the Thrift Shop? Yes No

8 Activity Sheets for Health

Unit 8 Health Tapescripts

A Case of Nerves
Focused Listening I / Dictionary, pp. 66–67
(No Activity Sheet)

Look at pages 66 and 67 in your dictionary. Listen to Nurse Fine talk to a nervous patient on the phone.
Point to the situations she describes.

Now Mr. Juarez, don't be nervous. I know you haven't been to our office before. * The **doctor** is very good and will explain everything, but let me tell you exactly what will happen when you get here.* When you come into the waiting room, you'll go directly to our **receptionist**, Hilda, at the **receptionist's** window. Hilda Garcia. * You said you have insurance, so **show** your **insurance card** at the reception desk.* We ask all our patients to **print** their names on everything. It makes the record keeping much easier.* We will also ask you to **sign** several papers, so come a little early for your appointment.* You will have to **wait** for a few minutes. I know, but everyone waits at a doctor's office.* Dr. Hansen is very busy. Then I'll **weigh** you on the scale. I'll write your weight and height on your records. Don't worry, I'm sure you are fine.* In the examining room the doctor will come in and **examine** you. No, this doesn't take long. Right, the doctor always listens to your heart. Yes, Doctor Hansen is a woman, but there's no need to be embarrassed.* Uh-huh, the Doctor does **give injections** sometimes, but don't worry. It's all over very quickly.* If you don't feel well, I'll **take your temperature**. Do you think you have a fever? No fever? That's good.* Yes, when you are sick the doctor usually **writes a prescription** for some medication. She does that in her office.* Now, Mr. Juarez are you ready to make an appointment? Good. How about this afternoon at 3:00? 3:00's not good? What about 4:00? 4:30?

Everybody's Out!
Focused Listening II / Activity Sheet, p. 111

Listen to the secretary talking about the office staff.
Circle the correct picture.

1. Yes, Ms. Goldman? Sam Waters? Oh, he just called. He has a terrible **backache**. He says he can't come in to work for two days. He has to stay in bed and get some rest. I know we really need him around here.

2. No, I'm sorry Ms. Goldman. Juan can't come in today. He has a **fever**. Yes, it's a high fever, he has a temperature of 102°.

3. Yes, Ms. Goldman? Yes, that's right. There will be no mail service this morning. The mail clerk's out today. Yes, I know he just had a vacation, but he **burned himself** on the barbeque grill. Yes, that kind of burn is very painful.

4. Hello? Oh hello, Kim. What's the matter? You have a bad **rash**? Oh that's too bad. You have to go to the doctor? Okay. I'll tell Ms. Goldman. Feel better.

5. Hello. May I help you? Oh, hello Margot. What? You're going to the dentist? But you didn't tell me. Oh, I see, you had to make an appointment this morning. Yes, I'm sure it's a bad **toothache**. All right, I'll tell Ms. Goldman. I don't think she'll be happy.

6. Excuse me, Ms. Goldman? I'm sorry to disturb you, but both Margot and Kim just called to tell me that they won't be in. Oh? really? The executive director called you? She has a **cold**? Well I guess that leaves just you and me, Ms. Goldman. Everyone else is sick. Oh, everyone but Sheila. She comes in at 9:00.

7. Uh, Ms. Goldman. I'm sorry to tell you this but Sheila just called and she can't come in to work today either. She has a bad **stomachache**. She thinks it was the fish at lunch yesterday.

8. Come to think of it... I had some of that fish too. Oh dear, Ms. Goldman, I'm not feeling very well. I think I'm going to **faint**. Aieeee....

Get Him a Band-Aid
Focused Listening II / Activity Sheet, p. 112

Listen to the doctor talking to the patients.
Follow the directions on your paper.

1. Mr. Johnson, show me your hand. Now, now... it's just a little **cut**. Let's get you a... (**Band-Aid**)

2. Okay, Ricky. I know you need something cold on that **swollen ankle**. Let me get you an... (**ice pack**)

3. My goodness, Mrs. Rodriguez, your forehead is very hot. I think you have a **fever**. Now where did I put that... (**thermometer**)

4. Okay, Ming. Sit up here on the table and let's check that **rash**. Oh, it looks nasty. Let me put on some... (**ointment**)

5. I think I'm going to take an X ray of that arm Ms. Rollin. It must be **broken**. We're going to need to put it in a... (**cast**)

6. Oh my, Mrs. Lee. Your **blood pressure** is way too high. I'm going to get you a new prescription for your blood pressure... (**pills**)

Listen to the secretary talking about the office staff.
Circle the correct picture.

1.

a.

b.

2.

a.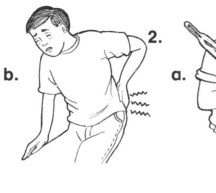

b.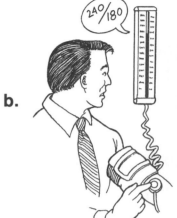

240/180

3.

a.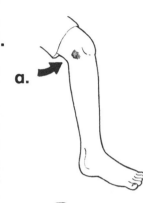

b.

4.

a.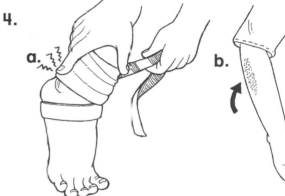

b.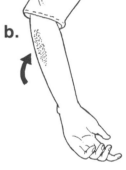

5.

a.

b.

6.

a.

b.

7.

a.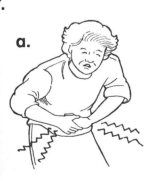

b.

8.

a.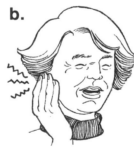

b.

Get Him a Band-Aid*

Focused Listening II/Teacher's Notes, p. 3/Dictionary, p. 64–65

- **Fold your paper on the dotted line.**
- **Listen to the doctor talking to the patients.**
- **Circle the correct word.**

1. crutches	cotton balls	(a Band-Aid)
2. ointment	ice pack	injection
3. bandage	thermometer	heating pad
4. thermometer	ointment	wheelchair
5. cast	Band-Aid	walker
6. pills	cotton balls	crutches

------------------------- FOLD HERE -------------------------

- **Listen again and match the patient to the ailment.**

1. Mr. Johnson	___	**a.** fever
2. Ricky	___	**b.** broken arm
3. Mrs. Rodriguez	___	**c.** high blood pressure
4. Ming	___	**d.** swollen ankle
5. Ms. Rollin	___	**e.** rash
6. Mrs. Lee	1	**f.** cut

* tapescript on p. 110

You're Catching a Cold

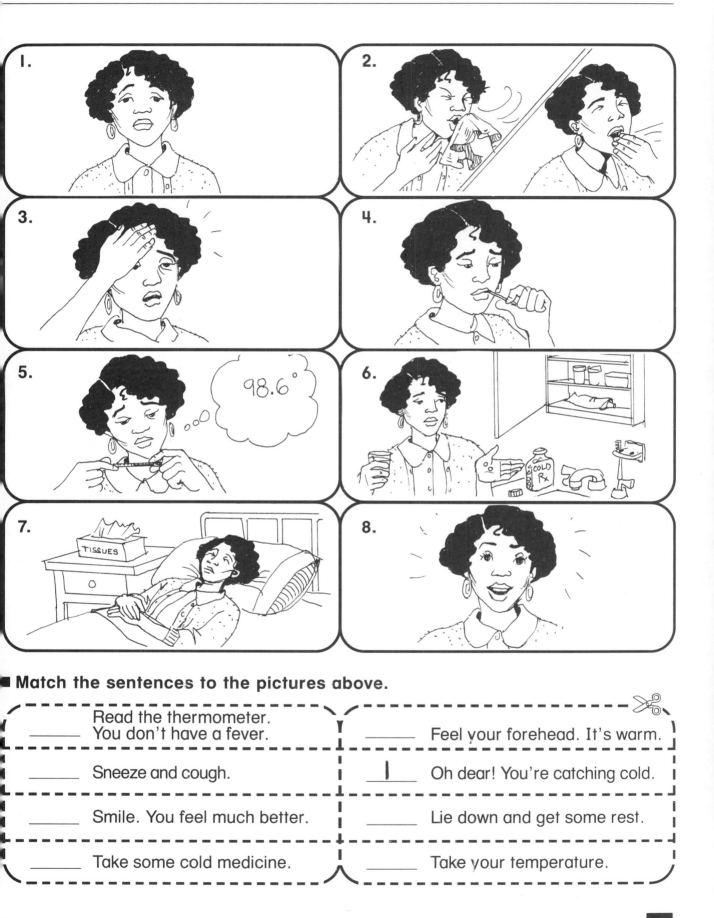

1.

2.

3.

4.

5. 98.6°

6. COLD Rx

7. TISSUES

8.

■ **Match the sentences to the pictures above.**

_____ Read the thermometer.
_____ You don't have a fever.

_____ Sneeze and cough.

_____ Smile. You feel much better.

_____ Take some cold medicine.

_____ Feel your forehead. It's warm.

__I__ Oh dear! You're catching cold.

_____ Lie down and get some rest.

_____ Take your temperature.

1. ■ Sit with a partner. Don't look at your partner's paper.
   ■ Look at the ad from DrugMore Pharmacy.
   ■ Answer your partner's questions about the prices.

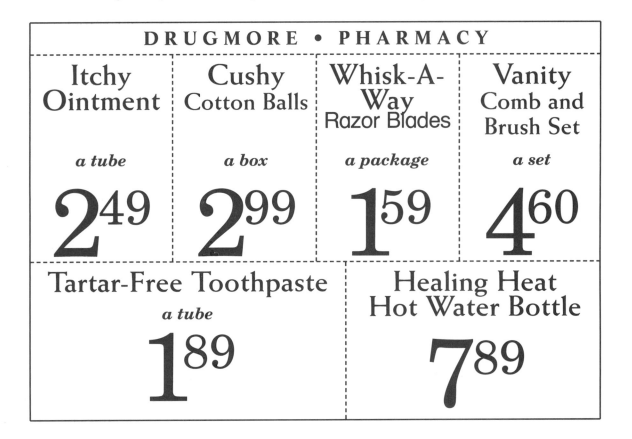

DRUGMORE • PHARMACY

Itchy Ointment	Cushy Cotton Balls	Whisk-A-Way Razor Blades	Vanity Comb and Brush Set
a tube	*a box*	*a package*	*a set*
2⁴⁹	2⁹⁹	1⁵⁹	4⁶⁰

Tartar-Free Toothpaste	Healing Heat Hot Water Bottle
a tube	
1⁸⁹	7⁸⁹

2. ■ Ask your partner for the prices of the sale items on the list at the right.
   ■ Ask questions, such as:

   How much is the _____ ?
   How much are the _____ ?

   ■ Write the prices on the list.

> ointment $2.49
> cotton balls $2.99
> thermometer
> Band-Aids
> ear drops
> shampoo

How Much Is the Ointment?

Info Exchange/Teacher's Notes, p. 5/Dictionary, pp. 61, 54–65

1. ■ **Sit with a partner. Don't look at your partner's paper.**
   ■ **Ask your partner for the prices of the sale items on the list at the right.**
   ■ **Ask questions, such as:**

   How much is the _____ *?*

   How much are the _____ *?*

   ■ **Write the prices on the list.**

ointment	$2.49
cotton balls	$2.99
razor blades	
comb and brush set	
hot water bottle	
toothpaste	

2. ■ **Look at the ad from Greene's Drugstore.**
   ■ **Answer your partner's questions about the prices.**

GREENE'S ♥ DRUGS

Itchy Ointment	**Cushy** Cotton Balls	**Kiddie** Band-Aids	**Silky** Shampoo
a tube	*a box*	*a box*	*a bottle*
2⁴⁹	2⁹⁹	1¹⁹	3⁵⁰

Fever Free Digital Thermometer	**Ear Clear Drops**
	a bottle
10⁹⁹	1²⁹

Do You Exercise?

Interview/Teacher's Notes, p. 7/Dictionary, pp. 64, 66–67

- **Read the questions and write your answers.**
- **Ask and answer the questions with your partner.**
- **Write your partner's answers.**

	My Answers	My Partner's Answers
1. Do you exercise?		
2. Do you take medicine?		
3. Do you have medical insurance?		
4. Do you see a doctor once a year?		
5. How do you feel?		

- **Circle the correct words.**

You	Your partner
1. I exercise. / don't exercise.	1. He / She exercises. / doesn't exercise.
2. I take / don't take medicine.	2. He / She takes / doesn't take medicine.
3. I have / don't have medical insurance.	3. He / She has / doesn't have medical insurance.
4. I see / don't see a doctor once a year.	4. He / She sees / doesn't see a doctor once a year.
5. I feel okay. / great. / terrible.	5. He / She feels okay. / great. / terrible.

Health

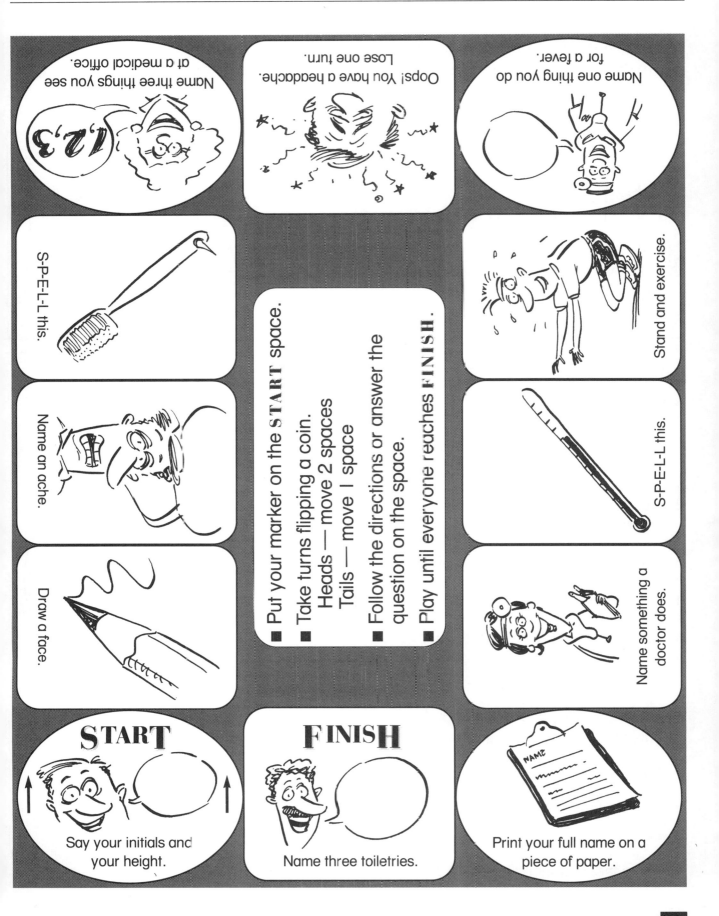

Name three things you see at a medical office.

Oops! You have a headache. Lose one turn.

Name one thing you do for a fever.

S-P-E-L-L this.

Stand and exercise.

Name an ache.

S-P-E-L-L this.

Draw a face.

Name something a doctor does.

- Put your marker on the **START** space.
- Take turns flipping a coin.
  Heads — move 2 spaces
  Tails — move 1 space
- Follow the directions or answer the question on the space.
- Play until everyone reaches **FINISH**.

START

Say your initials and your height.

FINISH

Name three toiletries.

Print your full name on a piece of paper.

Puppet Patients

LEA Picture/Teacher's Notes, p. 10/Dictionary, p. 58–59

■ **You are going to make a puppet patient.**
■ **Your teacher will tape your puppet to the board like this:**

■ **Then you will talk, write, and read about the experience.**

DIRECTIONS:

1. Get these things from your teacher: <u>construction paper,</u>
   a pair of <u>scissors,</u> a <u>popsicle stick,</u> <u>tape,</u> and <u>9 brad clips</u>.

2. Cut out a head, a body, two arms, two hands, two legs,
   and two feet from the construction paper.

3. Attach the parts of the body with brads.

4. Draw a face on your puppet and give it a name.

5. Look at pages 62 and 63 in your dictionary.
   Write your puppet's ache, pain, or injury
   on the correct part of the body.

6. Tape your puppet patient up on the board.
   Talk about all the patients with your classmates.

7. Describe the patients to your teacher.
   (Your teacher will write what you say on the board.)

8. Look at the sentences on the board and copy them.

9. Read the sentences to a classmate.

■ **Read the information on the labels.**
■ **Circle these words:**

blood pressure   daily   Doctor   drops earache   pills   prescription   times

DRUGMORE • PHARMACY
Prescription No. 579221
Dr. Silver
Patient: Joe Yung
Apply two drops every four
hours for earache.
Do not use after 7/95

GREENE'S DRUGS
Prescription No. 468921
Dr. White
Patient: Jane Fine
Take two pills two times daily
for high blood pressure.
Refill 2 times
Expires 9/95

DO NOT DRINK
ALCOHOLIC
BEVERAGES
WHEN TAKING THIS
MEDICATION

■ **Write the missing information.**

1. Joe Yung has an __earache__ .

2. His prescription is for ear _____ .

3. He has to take _____ drops every _____ hours.

4. He has to throw the medicine away in July, _____ .

5. Jane Fine has _____ _____ _____ .

6. Her prescription is for blood pressure _____ .

7. She has to take the pills _____ times daily.

8. She can't drink _____ with these pills.

9. She can refill the prescription _____ times.

10. She has to throw out the medicine in _____ , 1995.

We're Having a Health Fair

Narrative Reading/Teacher's Notes, p. 12/Dictionary, pp. 62–67

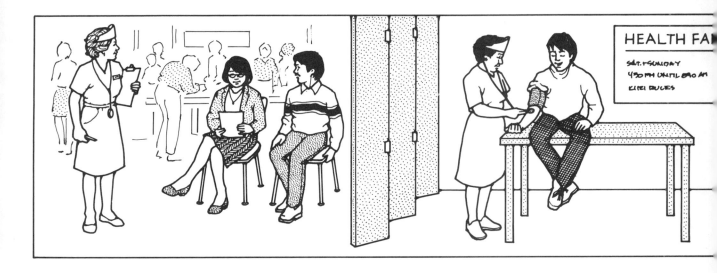

We're having a Health Fair at our adult school. Every student is getting a free examination and information on first aid and health care. Students fill out a form with their name, address, and phone number. Then they wait for a nurse to call them in for their examination.

There are five nurses at different tables. One nurse checks students' blood pressure. Another nurse weighs students and measures their height. Three other nurses give students a blood test. We also have first aid demonstrations for minor injuries.

The students can't get prescriptions or injections at the fair, but they do get good information and advice. Everyone comes to our Health Fair—the students, the teachers, even the school nurse!

■ Circle the answer.

1. The Health Fair is at the hospital.   True   (False)

2. The students fill out forms first.   True   False

3. The nurses take the students' temperature.   True   False

4. The nurses check the students' blood pressure.   True   False

5. There are first aid demonstrations.   True   False

6. You can get a prescription at the Health Fair.   True   False

9 Activity Sheets for The Community

■ Working at Central Bank
Focused Listening I/Dictionary, p. 70
(No Activity Sheet)

Look at page 70 in your dictionary. Listen to Ron Lopez talking about working at Central Bank. Point to the pictures you hear him talking about.

Hello, I'm Ron Lopez. I'm the **security guard** here at Central Bank. That's me in the uniform.* Usually I stand by the door but today I'm standing near Barbara, she's the new **teller**. The one in the yellow dress? Today is her first day at work. She's a little nervous.* Her first customer made a **deposit**. When she took the money, she did fine.* But her second customer made a **withdrawal,** and I could see her hands shake. She counted the money out three times.* Lucky for her, today we have a short **line**. Yesterday the line was very long.* Now, there's Mr. Matsubara at the **cash machine**. He doesn't like to wait. The cash machine is perfect for people like him.* Oh, and look at that woman at the **drive-thru window**. What do you think? Isn't she beautiful? It's her second time here today.* About an hour ago, she lost a **check** when she came in and I found it. There was her **signature** on it at the bottom and today's **date** at the top, January 22. The **amount** was for $150.00. I called her right away. "Honey," I said, "When you were here this morning you dropped our check for the electric company. If we don't get that in, they'll turn off our lights!" I love my wife, but she's always losing things.

■ Flowers for Valentine's Day
Focused Listening II/Activity Sheet, p. 123

Listen to the florist talking to her delivery person. Follow the directions on your paper.

1. You have a lot of flowers to deliver, Ravi. This is our best Valentine's Day ever! Take the **red** roses over to First City **Bank**. They're for Stella Rosen.

2. The **yellow** daisies are for Judge Harris over at the **courthouse**. Her husband always sends daisies.

3. Gina Sarducci is getting the **pink** carnations. She works at the **mall**, in the candy store.

4. See that big bouquet of **white** mums? That goes over to a teacher at the **school**, Mrs. Paul. Her daughter ordered them for her. Isn't that nice? Mums for Mom.

5. Ravi, be careful with that little arrangement of **orange** tiger lilies. It's going to Susan Haskell at the **bookstore**. Her boyfriend Henry likes them the best.

6. Now the **purple** orchids are really special. They came all the way from Hawaii. They go to the **police station** for the captain's secretary, a nice lady named Marna Skyler.

7. The big **green** plant is going to the new **bakery**, Breadworks. It's not for Valentine's Day. It's for good luck. They've just opened.

8. Don't touch that big vase of **blue** violets. They stay right here at the Fancy **Florist**. My husband always sends me blue violets on Valentine's Day because we met right here!

■ Heroes in the News
Focused Listening II/Activity Sheet, p. 124

Listen to the radio announcer. Follow the directions on your paper.

Welcome to "Heroes in the News."

1. **Hurricane** Roger stayed about three miles off the coast of Georgia last **Sunday** before going out to sea. Many ham radio operators helped the small boats.

2. In New York City, a bank **robbery** by computer was discovered last **Thursday** at State National Bank. Sam Jacobs, a bank teller, discovered the robbery. Sam received a $500 reward for his assistance.

3. A big **tornado** went through Kansas and Nebraska last **Friday**. There were no injuries because of the tremendous efforts of the folks at Kansas Tornado Watch.

4. Moving to the South, there was a small **flood** in the Mississippi delta on **Saturday**. No one was hurt because of the flood warnings put out on WKPL, a local radio station.

5. A bus and a train did not have an **accident** last **Tuesday** near San Antonio. The bus driver and his passengers pushed the bus off the train tracks just in time. Rubio Gonzalez used quick thinking. He's a great bus driver!

6. And on the West coast, there was a small **earthquake** near Solvang last **Wednesday**. No injuries were reported but power lines were down. All seven members of the Shulmer family directed traffic next to the power lines. Their picture was in the local papers.

7. And the Central City Poison Center in California saved the life of two-year-old Rina Harris on **Sunday**. She **swallowed poison** but is fine now.

8. On **Monday** there was an oil well **fire** off the coast of California. Damage was light due to quick thinking on the part of the Coast Guard who alerted the fire fighters.

9. Four year-old Harry Bonzini saved his grandmother's life last **Thursday** when he dialed 911. His grandmother suffered a small **heart attack**, but the paramedics got his call and came four minutes later. Harry got a big kiss from his grandmother.

10. And on the light side, in Los Angeles, a dog named Cookie got a special dinner when he rescued a cat named Maui last **Saturday**. Maui almost **drowned** in the family swimming pool and Cookie barked until someone came. That's it for "Heroes in the News".

Flowers for Valentine's Day*

Focused Listening II / Teacher's Notes, p. 3 / Dictionary, pp. 78–79

■ **Fold your paper on the dotted line.**
■ **Listen and circle the correct location.**

I. train station	(bank)	church
2. courthouse	park	department store
3. school	mall	city hall
4. movie theatre	school	bus station
5. supermarket	bakery	bookstore
6. police station	gym	bus station
7. DMV	park	bakery
8. office building	florist	fire station

- FOLD HERE -

■ **Listen again for the colors of the flowers.**
■ **Write the correct letter next to the number.**

I. __C__	**a.** green
2._____	**b.** orange
3._____	**c.** red
4._____	**d.** pink
5._____	**e.** blue
6._____	**f.** purple
7._____	**g.** yellow
8._____	**h.** white

* tapescript on p. 122

■ **Fold your paper on the dotted line.**

■ **Listen and number the news events.**

_____ flood   _____ accident   _____ earthquake   _____ robbery

__1__ hurricane   _____ drown   _____ tornado   _____ fire

                 _____ swallow poison   _____ have a heart attack

- FOLD HERE -

■ **Listen again and make a (✓) under the correct day of the week.**

	Sun.	Mon.	Tues.	Wed.	Thurs.	Fri.	Sat.
1.	✓						
2.							
3.							
4.							
5.							
6.							
7.							
8.							
9.							
10.							

* tapescript on p. 122

Paying a Telephone Bill

TPR Sequence/Teacher's Notes, p. 4/Dictionary, pp. 70–71

■ Match the sentences to the pictures above.

_____ Put a stamp on the envelope and mail it.

_____ Go to the post office.

_____ Look over the bill.

_____ Stand in line.

_____ Buy a money order and a stamp.

_____ Put the money order and payment stub in an envelope.

___1___ It's time to pay the phone bill.

_____ Sign your name on the money order.

1. ■ Sit with a partner. Don't show your paper to your partner.

■ Tell your partner what these people are doing:

   Ted   *Rita*   *Tina*   *Sook*

2. ■ Listen to your partner tell you what these people are doing:

   Boris   *Leo*   *Sarkis*   *Elena*

■ Write the names in the correct spaces.

B

I. ■ Sit with a partner. Don't show your paper to your partner.
■ Listen to your partner tell you what these people are doing:
Ted   Rita   Tina   Sook
■ Write the names in the correct spaces.

2. ■ Tell your partner what these people are doing:
Boris   Leo   Sarkis   Elena

Mixer / Teacher's Notes, p. 6 / Dictionary, pp. 68–69

- **Write the missing letters in the words.**
- **Walk around the room. Ask and answer the questions.**
- **Write a different name in each box.**

1. Do you live near a p o s t o f f i c e?

   YES ——————————   NO ——————————

2. Do you live near a c h _ _ c _ ?

   YES ——————————   NO ——————————

3. Do you live near a m _ _ l?

   YES ——————————   NO ——————————

4. Do you live near a p _ _ k?

   YES ——————————   NO ——————————

5. Do you live near a s c _ _ _ l?

   YES ——————————   NO ——————————

6. Do you live near a b _ k _ r y?

   YES ——————————   NO ——————————

Board Game/Teacher's Notes, p. 8/Dictionary, pp. 68–75

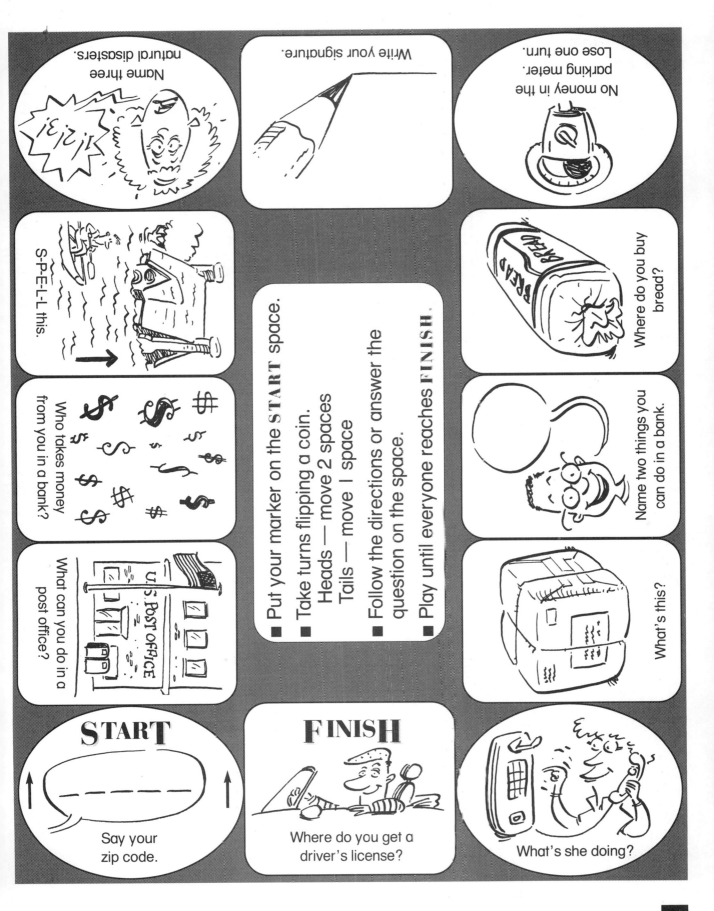

Name three natural disasters.

Write your signature.

No money in the parking meter. Lose one turn.

S-P-E-L-L this.

Where do you buy bread?

Who takes money from you in a bank?

- Put your marker on the **START** space.
- Take turns flipping a coin.
  Heads — move 2 spaces
  Tails — move 1 space
- Follow the directions or answer the question on the space.
- Play until everyone reaches **FINISH**.

Name two things you can do in a bank.

What can you do in a post office?

What's this?

START

Say your zip code.

FINISH

Where do you get a driver's license?

What's she doing?

- ■ **Look at the picture below.**
- ■ **Describe the situation to your teacher.**

■ **Copy the description.**

_____

_____

_____

_____

_____

_____

_____

City Services

Life Skills Reading/Teacher's Notes, p. 11/Dictionary, pp. 74–75

■ **Read the telephone directory below.**

■ **Circle these words:**

ambulance	**emergency**	**fire**	**library**	**poison**	**police**

GOVERNMENT OFFICES—CITY
City of Blue Bay
AMBULANCE   9 – 1 – 1
City Hall
500 Central Av.   555–3427
City Manager   555–3423
Blue Bay Stop Crime   555–3827
Information Referral   555–4833
Finance   555–3490
Fire Dept.   150 S. 4th   555–9000
   EMERGENCY CALLS   9 – 1 – 1
   North Area   555–9005
   South Area   555–9009
Parks and Recreation   555–6833
POISON CONTROL   555–5000
Police Department   525 Central Av.
   EMERGENCY CALLS   9 – 1 – 1
   Report Crime   555–7000
   Records   555–7005
Public Library   555–4991
Swimming Pool   555–3728
Visitor Information   555–3488
Water Department   555–8911

■ **Write the telephone numbers:**

1. If someone swallows poison, dial __555-5000__ .

2. If there's a fire on your street, dial _____ .

3. If you want to call the park, dial _____ .

4. If you want to report a crime, dial _____ .

5. If you need an ambulance, dial _____ .

6. If you want to call the swimming pool, dial _____ .

7. If you want to call the water department, dial _____ .

8. If you want to call the library, dial _____ .

GRAND STREET

I love driving a bus. My "regulars" at the end of the day are very nice.
Mrs. Lee is a florist. She waits in front of the newsstand on 4th Street.
Bob Becker is a security guard at the mall. He always stands on the sidewalk
at 8th Street. Odilia Solares, a bank teller, waits at the corner of 10th Street.
Sometimes, Odilia doesn't take the bus. She likes to look at the clothes
in the windows or buy a few groceries on the way home. Mary Ford always sits
on the bench at the intersection of 11th and Grand. She's a postal worker.
She walks all day long.

And me? At the end of the day my husband picks me up at the bus station.
He drives and I look out for pedestrians!

■ **Draw a line to complete the sentence.**

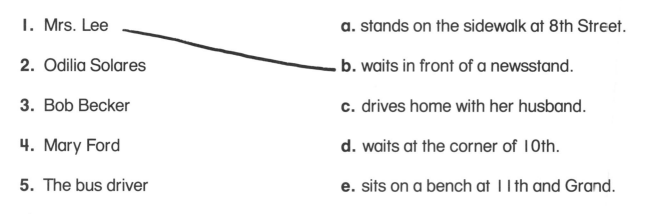

1. Mrs. Lee   a. stands on the sidewalk at 8th Street.

2. Odilia Solares   b. waits in front of a newsstand.

3. Bob Becker   c. drives home with her husband.

4. Mary Ford   d. waits at the corner of 10th.

5. The bus driver   e. sits on a bench at 11th and Grand.

10 Activity Sheets for Transportation

Unit 10 Transportation Tapescripts

■ Hurry! Our Plane Is Leaving!

Focused Listening I/Dictionary, pp. 80–81
(No Activity Sheet)

Look at pages 80 and 81 in your dictionary. Listen to Barbara and Rob Johnson as they run through the airport. Point to the pictures you hear them talking about.

Rob: Let's hurry, Barbara. We can't miss that plane! It's our first vacation in three years!

Barbara: Wait! Aren't you checking the bags?

Rob: We don't have time to **check the bags**!* Do you have your **boarding pass**?

Barbara: My boarding pass? It's right here.*

Rob: Give it to the security guard. He has to see it at the **security check**. I'll put our bags on the conveyor belt.

Barbara: (buzzer) Oh no! You set off the alarm. Take the change out of your pocket.*

Rob: Okay, okay. Let's go. Which way is it?

Barbara: This way. We're almost there. I see the plane. The **pilot** is already in the cockpit.*

Rob: What **gate** are we at?

Barbara: Gate 12. See? There's the **flight attendant** taking the tickets. Oh no! I can't find my **ticket**! Oh, here it is, in my hand. Let's get in line.*

Rob: Finally, we made it. We can relax now! We are going to **leave** this old city! Tonight we'll be in Italy!*

Barbara: Relax? I can't relax! We're going to Italy and we don't speak Italian. How are we going to the hotel? Who is going to **meet** us?

Rob: Don't worry. The hotel driver knows our name. He is going to meet us with a big sign that says, "Johnson." I'll **shake his hand** and away we'll go!

■ Going to Work

Focused Listening II/Activity Sheet, p. 135

Listen to Paulo describe his route. Follow the directions on your paper.

1. I always ride my bike to work. I like to keep track of the time. That's how I know I ride **away from** my apartment at 6:30 every morning.

2. By 6:33 I'm usually riding **up** Ross Hill. It's a long climb, and I put my bike into low gear.

3. If I ride fast, I reach the top in about seven minutes or so, and at 6:40 I'm on my way **down** the hill.

4. At the bottom of the hill is the Big Oak Tunnel. I go **through** the tunnel by 6:45. It's very pretty. I can usually see the sun coming through the far end.

5. I ride straight for a while. Then I come to Highway 62. I'm going **over** Highway 62 by 6:55. When I see all the cars on the highway, I'm glad I'm on my bike.

6. After I pass Highway 62, I get to Ferry Way. It's a big street. Usually I walk my bike **across** the traffic so everyone will see me. I cross Ferry Way at 7:01.

7. At 7:10 I ride **into** the gas station at the corner of Central and Marsh. That's perfect because I don't have to be at work until 7:30 and I like to come early.

8. At exactly 4:30 in the afternoon I ride **out of** the gas station and I'm on my way home. My job? Can you guess? I pump gas at the gas station! Fill 'er up?

■ Car Draw

Focused Listening II/Activity Sheet, p. 136

Look at the pictures of the cars and follow the directions on your paper.

Look at picture A.

1. Put a 1 on the hood.
2. Put a 2 on the right headlight.
3. Put a 3 on the left headlight.
4. Put a 4 on the windshield.
5. Put a 5 on the left tire.
6. Put a 6 on the right tire.

Look at picture B.

7. Put a 7 on the license plate.
8. Put an 8 on the gas tank.
9. Put a 9 on the trunk.

Look at picture C.

10. Put a 10 on the steering wheel.
11. Put an 11 on the dashboard.
12. Put a 12 on the brake.
13. Put a 13 on the ignition.
14. Put a 14 on the accelerator.
15. Put a 15 on the seat belt.

■ **Fold your paper on the dotted line.**
■ **Listen and write the correct number.**

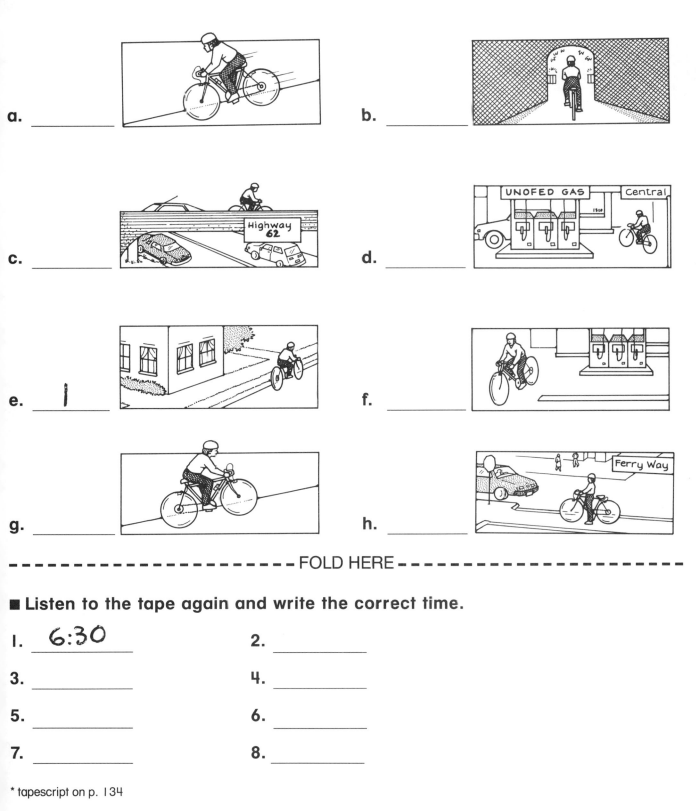

a. _____

b. _____

c. _____

d. _____

e. ___I___

f. _____

g. _____

h. _____

- FOLD HERE -

■ **Listen to the tape again and write the correct time.**

1. __6:30__   2. _____

3. _____   4. _____

5. _____   6. _____

7. _____   8. _____

* tapescript on p. 134

■ Listen and write the numbers on the parts of the car.

a.

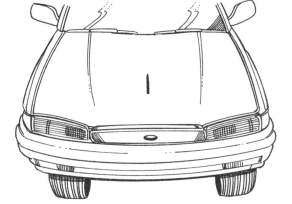

b.

c.

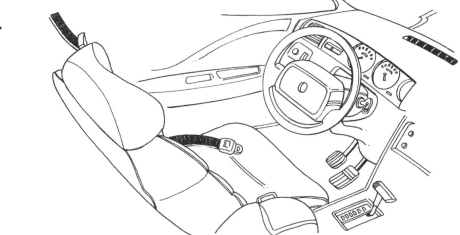

* tapescript on p. 134

A Friendly Visit

TPR Sequence/Teacher's Notes, p. 4/Dictionary, pp. 76–81

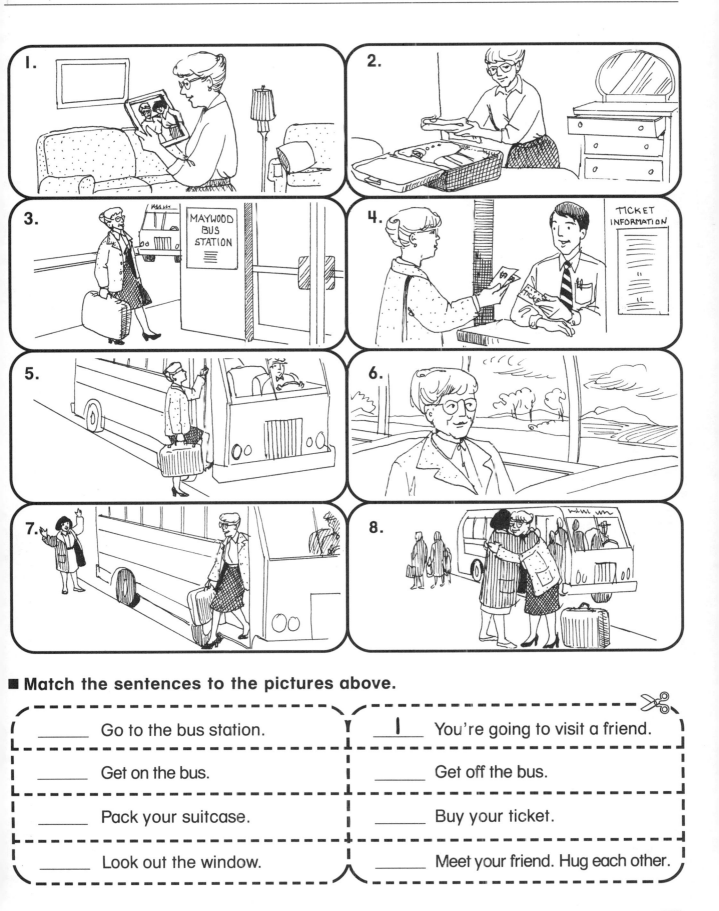

■ Match the sentences to the pictures above.

_____ Go to the bus station.	**I** You're going to visit a friend.
_____ Get on the bus.	_____ Get off the bus.
_____ Pack your suitcase.	_____ Buy your ticket.
_____ Look out the window.	_____ Meet your friend. Hug each other.

1. Sit with a partner. Don't show your paper to your partner.
   Look at the pictures.
   Ask your partner questions, such as:
   How much is the _____?
   Write the answers on the price tags.

2. Look at the pictures.
   Answer your partner's questions about the prices.

1. ☐ Sit with a partner. Don't show your paper to your partner.
   ☐ Look at the pictures.
   ☐ Answer your partner's questions about the prices.

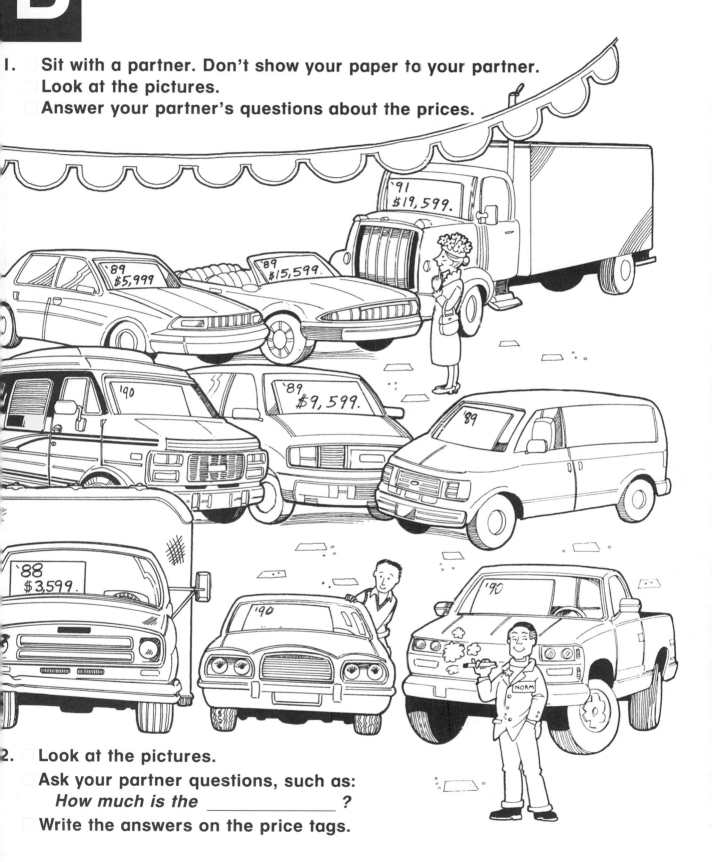

2. ☐ Look at the pictures.
   ☐ Ask your partner questions, such as:
      How much is the _____ ?
   ☐ Write the answers on the price tags.

What Can You Do?

Interview/Teacher's Notes, p. 7/Dictionary, p. 76

- ■ **Read the questions and mark your answers.**
- ■ **Ask and answer the questions with your partner.**
- ■ **Write your partner's answers.**

	My Answers	My Partner's Answers
1. Can you drive a car?		
2. Can you ride a bicycle?		
3. Can you ride a motorcycle?		
4. Can you drive a truck?		
5. Can you fly a plane?		

- ■ **Circle the correct words.**

You			Your partner		
1. I	can can't	drive a car.	1. He She	can can't	drive a car.
2. I	can can't	ride a bicycle.	2. He She	can can't	ride a bicycle.
3. I	can can't	ride a motorcycle.	3. He She	can can't	ride a motorcycle.
4. I	can can't	drive a truck.	4. He She	can can't	drive a truck.
5. I	can can't	fly a plane.	5. He She	can can't	fly a plane.

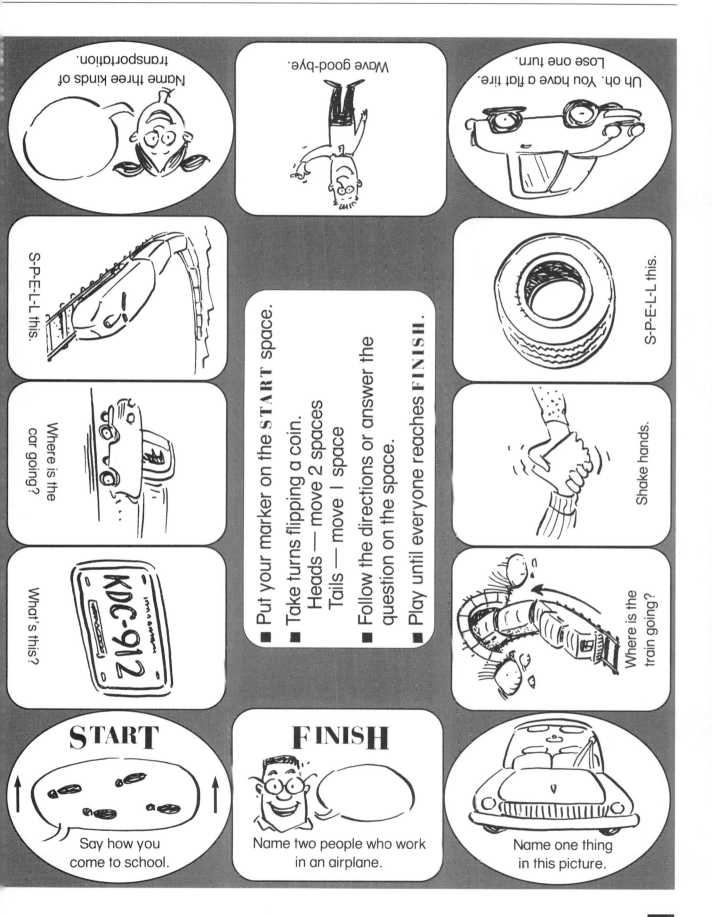

Name three kinds of transportation.

Wave good-bye.

Uh oh. You have a flat tire. Lose one turn.

S-P-E-L-L this.

S-P-E-L-L this.

Where is the car going?

Shake hands.

What's this?

KDC-912

Where is the train going?

- Put your marker on the **START** space.
- Take turns flipping a coin.
  Heads — move 2 spaces
  Tails — move 1 space
- Follow the directions or answer the question on the space.
- Play until everyone reaches **FINISH**.

START

Say how you come to school.

FINISH

Name two people who work in an airplane.

Name one thing in this picture.

LEA Picture/Teacher's Notes, p. 9/Dictionary, p. 76–77

- **■ Look at the picture below.**
- **■ Describe the situation to your teacher.**

■ Copy the description.

_____

_____

_____

_____

_____

_____

_____

Airport Signs

_ife Skills Reading/Teacher's Notes, p. I I/Dictionary, pp. 80–81

Read the signs below.

Circle these words:

| arrivals | baggage | passengers | taxi | transportation |

a. BAGGAGE CLAIM

b. SECURITY CHECK NO EXIT

c. PASSENGERS ONLY BEYOND THIS POINT

d. LOADING ZONE NO PARKING

e. GROUND TRANSPORTATION

f. TAXI STAND

g. PURCHASE TICKETS · CHECK IN

h. ARRIVALS

Write the correct letter.

1. __e__ You can find a bus here.

2. _____ You can't leave your car here.

3. _____ Drive this way to meet people.

4. _____ You need a ticket for the airplane to go here.

5. _____ Security checks your carry-on bags here.

6. _____ You can buy a ticket here.

7. _____ You get your luggage here.

8. _____ You can get a taxi here.

Is This a Vacation?

Narrative Reading/Teacher's Notes, p. 12/Dictionary, pp. 76–79

Every summer Ed and Nancy Reed take a car trip. This year they are going to Texas. They always leave early in the morning. The night before they go, Ed Reed always washes the car windshield. He checks the battery under the hood. He also checks the headlights. Usually he fills the gas tank. Nancy Reed packs the suitcases. Their children, Emily, Sophie, and Ted, pack their toys. Then Ed packs everything in the trunk of the car.

The day of the trip everyone is always very excited. Emily and Sophie sit in the back. Ted sits in the child's seat between the two girls. Everyone wears a seat belt. Nancy always drives first.

Everyone is ready. Why aren't they going? Yesterday Ed forgot to get gas.

■ Circle the answer.

1. Where are they going?	Tennessee	(Texas)
2. Who packs the toys?	Nancy	the children
3. Who drives first?	Ed	Nancy
4. When do they leave the house?	in the morning	at night
5. Who packs the trunk?	Ed	Nancy
6. How many children do they have?	3	2

11 Activity Sheets for Work

Unit 11 Work Tapescripts

■ Hard Work
Focused Listening I/Dictionary, pp. 88–89
(No Activity Sheet)

Look at pages 88 and 89 in your dictionary. Listen to the people talking about their different jobs. Point to the work you hear each person describe.

Rose: Sheila, how's the new job?

Sheila: It's okay, Rose. I'm cutting hair in a little shop downtown. I like to **cut hair**. But sometimes it's hard work.

Rose: Oh, that's not so bad, you're young. Try working in a department store! When I was young, I liked to **sell** those beautiful **clothes**. I loved to sell. Now, I'm ready to retire.

Mike: I never want to retire. I love to **drive** my **truck** up and down the state. Of course, I used to **drive a taxi**. Now that's hard work, driving a taxi.

Karl: Oh Mike, that's not so hard. Just try to **deliver the mail**. Sure, it's great to deliver paychecks and birthday cards, but that junk mail! I hate it.

Oscar: You don't know about hard work. I used to be a construction foreman in San Salvador. I liked to **build houses**. But try to build a house here in the U.S., that's hard work.

Tony: So true, my friend. "Anna," I said to my wife, "I have to change professions." She said, "**Fix cars.** You like cars—fix cars." So I'm going to fix cars. Whaddya think of that?

Anna: (Yawn) Excuse me, Tony, I'm so tired. Those three kids wear me out. It's hard to **take care of children** all day.

Sam: Hard work can be a good thing. Sanitation work is not easy. I **collect the garbage** from your homes and your jobs, but it is good, honest work. It pays my bills.

Rose: Sam is right. Hard work is not so bad. Here's to us all and the work we do!

■ Taxicab for the Stars
Focused Listening II/Activity Sheet, p. 147

Listen and follow the directions on your paper.

1. I'm Louise DePalma and I'm a cabbie, a taxi driver. I drive all around this beautiful city. I get to take everyone, everywhere on Second Avenue. I get great tips, too. Usually about **$5** a ride.

2. Last week, for instance, I took the famous actress, Mona Mona, to the **beauty salon**. She tipped me **$4.00** for a two-minute ride. She looked better going into that salon than most of 'em looked coming out.

3. And not too long ago I took that famous opera singer, Placebo Domino, for a ride. He wanted me to take him down the street to the **drugstore**. His throat was very sore and he needed some medicine. Now, I know the guy was sick, but he only tipped me **50 cents**! Boy, was I mad.

4. Of course the best tip I got was from that famous actor, Paul Oldman. He tipped me a **20** for taking him to the **dentist's office**. He probably wanted to keep his smile looking good. I sure was smiling after I got his tip!

5. You know that important lawyer? Nelson Deli? He has an office on Second and Main. Funny thing is that every Friday he takes my cab to the **barbershop**. I get the same **$2.75** and he gets the same haircut!

6. I get more than tips on this job, y'know. Last year I picked up a fare, a dancer for the city dance company. I took him to the **fruit and vegetable market** on 14th and Second. (They love to eat all that healthy stuff.) Anyway, he didn't tip me because he **didn't have the money**. But that's okay. I married him anyway. What a job!

■ Bundles of Joy!
Focused Listening II/Activity Sheet, p. 148

Listen to the day-care workers talk to the children and each other. Circle the word that comes next.

1. Uh oh, Carlitos never cries in the morning. If he's **crying**, maybe he's wet. Go ahead and check his.. (**diaper**)

2. Tanya needs to **take a nap**, put her in the...(**crib**)

3. Oh, Georgie, you **drop**ped this again! You like to play, don't you? Here's your... (**rattle**)

4. I think Fanny's hungry. Susan, **pick** her **up** and give her a... (**bottle**).

5. Be careful when you feed little Johnny. He's wearing new clothes. Be sure to **put on** his... (**bib**)

6. It's time for Nancy to go outside. **Dress** her in the blue sweater and take her for a walk, but don't carry her! Put her in the... (**stroller**)

7. Susan, could you **rock** little Jenny for a while? She needs some quiet time. Put her in the... (**cradle**)

8. My goodness! Mikey **runs** everywhere Let's get him to sit down and play for a minute. Mikey! Here's your favorite... (**toy**)

■ **Fold your paper on the dotted line.**
■ **Listen to the taxi driver talk about her fares.**
■ **Match each person to the place where they went.**

1. taxi driver

2. actress

3. singer

4. actor

5. lawyer

6. dancer

___ **a.** dentist's office

___ **b.** drugstore

___ **c.** fruit and vegetable market

_l_ **d.** Second Avenue

___ **e.** beauty salon

___ **f.** barbershop

- - - - - - - - - - - - - - - - - - FOLD HERE -

Listen again and write the amount of the tip.

1. $5.00

2. _____

3. _____

4. _____

5. _____

6. _____

*tapescript on p. 146

Focused Listening II / Teacher's Notes, p. 3 / Dictionary, pp. 90–91

- ■ **Fold your paper on the dotted line.**
- ■ **Listen to the day-care workers talking to each other and the children.**
- ■ **Circle the word that comes next.**

1. bib	(diaper)	stroller
2. bib	rattle	crib
3. rattle	playpen	cradle
4. rattle	diaper	bottle
5. bib	pacifier	bottle
6. crib	stroller	playpen
7. cradle	playpen	rattle
8. diaper	toy	bib

- - - - - - - - - - - - - - - - - - - FOLD HERE - - - - - - - - - - - - - - - - - - -

- ■ **Listen again and write the missing word.**

cry	dress	drop	pick up	put on	rock	run	take a nap

1. Carlitos is ___cry___ ing because he's wet.

2. Tanya needs to _____ _____ _____ .

3. Georgie likes to _____ his rattle.

4. Susan has to _____ _____ Fanny.

5. They have to _____ a bib _____ Johnny.

6. Susan has to _____ Nancy in a blue sweater.

7. Susan needs to _____ Jenny.

8. Mikey loves to _____ .

* tapescript on p. 146

Painting a Room

TPR Sequence/Teacher's Notes, p. 4/Dictionary, p. 87

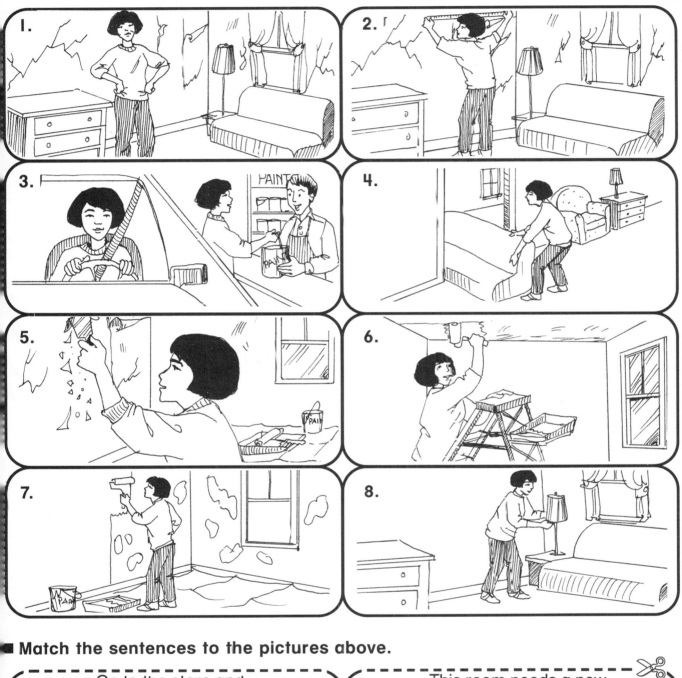

■ Match the sentences to the pictures above.

_____ Go to the store and buy some paint.	_1_ This room needs a new coat of paint!
_____ Put the furniture back in the room.	_____ Measure the room.
_____ Scrape off the old paint.	_____ Climb the ladder and paint the ceiling.
_____ Take out the furniture.	_____ Paint the walls.

Unit 11/Work **149**

I. ■ **Sit with a partner. Don't look at your partner's paper.**
   ■ **Look at the flyer for the occupational school.**
   ■ **Tell your partner the days and times of these classes:**
       dental assistant   house painting   word processing

★★

Learn a Job at Valley Trade School

★★★★★★★★★★★★ **Word Processing pays!** ★★★★★★★★★★★★
Learn a valuable office skill.
Classes offered T & Th
Eves. 6:30 – 10:00 p.m.

★★★★★★★★★★★★ **Paint Houses!** ★★★★★★★★★★★★
Be your own boss.
Train during the evenings
M – F   7 – 10 p.m.

★★★★★★★★★★★★ **Work in a Dentist's Office** ★★★★★★★★★★★★
Learn to be a Dental Assistant.
Saturday classes
from 10 a.m. – 1 p.m.

★★

2. ■ **Look at the list of classes below.**
   ■ **Listen to your partner and write the days and times on the list.**

Class	Day	Time
Hair Cutting	Mon. – Thurs.	
Meat Cutting		
Auto Mechanics		

When Does That Class Meet?

Info Exchange/Teacher's Notes, p. 5/Dictionary, pp. 82–89

1. ■ Sit with a partner. Don't look at your partner's paper.
   ■ Look at the list of classes below.
   ■ Listen to your partner and write the days and times on the list.

Class	Day	Time
Dental Assistant	Saturday	
Word Processing		
House Painting		

2. ■ Look at the flyer for the occupational school.
   ■ Tell your partner the days and times of these classes:
      auto mechanics   *hair cutting*   *meat cutting*

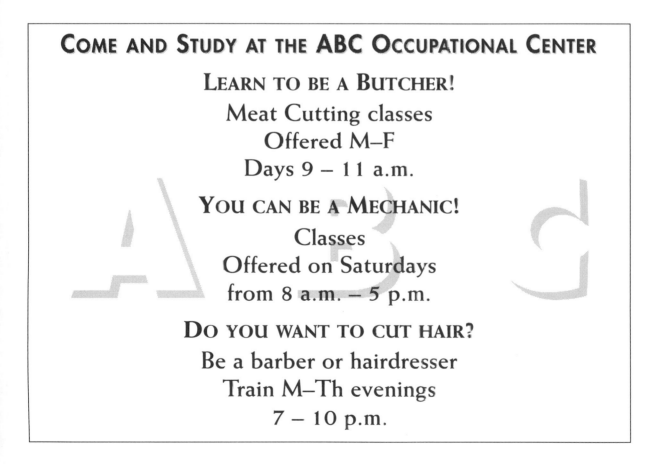

COME AND STUDY AT THE ABC OCCUPATIONAL CENTER

LEARN TO BE A BUTCHER!
Meat Cutting classes
Offered M–F
Days 9 – 11 a.m.

YOU CAN BE A MECHANIC!
Classes
Offered on Saturdays
from 8 a.m. – 5 p.m.

DO YOU WANT TO CUT HAIR?
Be a barber or hairdresser
Train M–Th evenings
7 – 10 p.m.

What Do Bus Drivers Do?

Mixer/Teacher's Notes, p. 6/Dictionary, pp. 82–89

■ **Write in the missing letters in the occupations.**

■ **Walk around the room. Ask and answer this question:**

   What do_____ do?

■ **Write your classmate's name in a box when the answer is correct.**

■ **Get names for all the squares.**

bus dr i ve r s _____	_ale_peo_le _____	but _ _ e _ s _____	co_s_ruc_io_ wo_ke_s _____
le_ _ e _ ca_ _ ie_s _____	sa_ita_ion w_ _ke_s _____	t_u_ _ dr_v_ _s _____	_a_ysi_ _ers _____
me _ _ani_s _____	g_o_ers _____	ha_rstyl_sts _____	t_ain _onduc_o_s _____

Board Game/Teacher's Notes, p. 8/Dictionary, pp. 82–89

Name something you see at a day-care center.

Name two workers who work outside.

Oops! You called in sick. Lose one turn.

S-P-E-L-L this occupation.

What is an occupation that starts with "B"?

Draw something you see at a construction site.

S-P-E-L-L this occupation.

Name an office job.

- Put your marker on the **START** space.
- Take turns flipping a coin.
  Heads — move 2 spaces
  Tails — move 1 space
- Follow the directions or answer the question on the space.
- Play until everyone reaches **FINISH**.

Name something he delivers.

START

Say your first name and your occupation.

FINISH

What's a job you want to do?

Draw something a driver drives.

LEA Picture/Teacher's Notes, p. 9/Dictionary, pp. 91–92

■ **Look at the pictures.**
■ **Tell the story to your teacher.**

■ **Copy the story.**

_____

_____

_____

_____

_____

_____

_____

_____

Job Ads

■ **Read the advertisements.**

■ **Circle these words:**

gardener	hour (hr.)	messenger	pays	word processor

Gardener Part time, mornings 8–12. 3.75/hr. Julio's gardening service Call days 555–1989	Word Processor Jobs 7.50/hr. Busy Dentist's office Full time and part time available Call between 1–3 M–F 555–1689	Messenger for Law Corporation Mail only, no packages. Need transportation. Pays $4/hr. Some eves. Apply M–F 1285 5th Street

■ **Circle the correct word or words.**

1. The gardener will work (four) / eight hours a day.

2. The pay is $15 / $4 an hour for the messenger.

3. The messenger will deliver mail. / packages.

4. The word processor job is in a dentist's / lawyer's office.

5. You call 555–1989 / 555–1689 to find out about the gardening job.

6. You can call at 4:00 / 2:00 for the word processor job.

Narrative Reading/Teacher's Notes, p. 12/Dictionary, pp. 82–86, 88–89

   Mornings on Main Street are very special. When I come home from the factory,
I see many people going to work. The construction workers start digging and
hammering at 7:00 a.m., before the lawyers and computer programmers get out of bed.
At 7:45, I usually see the office workers going to work. By 8:00, rain or shine,
the messengers are on their bicycles. The butcher shop, the barbershop, the library, and
the beauty salon are open for business at 9:00. Of course, not everyone goes to work
in the morning. Some of us have to work at night!

■ Circle the correct answer.

1. Who is telling the story?   a messenger   (a factory worker)

2. When does he come home from work?   in the afternoon   in the morning

3. When does he go to work?   in the afternoon   at night

4. What time does work begin at the construction site?   7:00 a.m.   8:00 a.m.

5. Who does the factory worker see at 7:45 a.m.?   the hairdresser   the office workers

6. Can you get a haircut at 8:00 a.m on Main Street?   Yes, you can.   No, you can't.

12 Activity Sheets for Recreation

* tapescript on p. 158

Unit 12 Recreation Tapescripts

■ Sports? I Love Sports!
Focused Listening I/Dictionary, pp. 92–93
(No Activity Sheet)

Look at pages 92 and 93 in your dictionary. Listen to the Director of Camp Valley High talking to Jerry Barish about getting a job at the camp. Point to the activities you hear them talking about.

Director: Welcome to Camp Valley High, Mr. Barish. We have many jobs available here if you like sports and outdoor activities. Do you like to **go hiking**? We always take hikes here.

Jerry: Hiking? No, I don't really like hiking. I'm not good going up hills.*

Director: Well, Jerry, do you like **sports**? We offer many sports to the children.

Jerry: Yes, yes, I do. I love sports.

Director: Well, how about tennis? Do you **play tennis**?

Jerry: Tennis? Well, no, not tennis. I'm not good with a racket.*

Director: How about football? Can you **play football**? We really need a good football coach.

Jerry: No, sorry. I don't play football. I'm not very fast.*

Director: No problem. You *are* tall. Do you **play basketball**?

Jerry: Not really. I'm not a good shooter and I can't dribble.*

Director: Maybe you could coach soccer? You just kick the ball when you **play soccer**. What do you say?

Jerry: I like soccer... in fact, I love soccer, but my feet are bad. I just can't run.*

Director: Well, I'm sure you **play baseball**. Everyone plays baseball. We don't have a baseball coach yet.

Jerry: Gosh, do I love baseball! But I never could hit the ball....*

Director: Uh... okay. You probably **go swimming**. Do you like the water? No rackets, no balls, no bats. Stay by the pool all day...

Jerry: That sounds great, but water gets in my nose when I swim.*

Director: Mr. Barish, I'm out of ideas. What do you like to do?

Jerry: Well, I love to **watch TV**, especially sports. And I love to **go to the movies**. I love movies about football and baseball. And the radio. I love to **listen to music**. I love all kinds of music. I even **play an instrument**— the piano.

Director: That's it! That's it! You can be our music teacher. We could use a good music teacher. What's your favorite song?

Jerry: "Take Me Out to the Ballgame!" I told you, I love sports!

(He sings "Take me out to the ballgame, take me out to the crowd...")

■ In Switzerland We Go Skiing
Focused Listening II/Activity Sheet, p. 159

Listen to the people talk about how they spend their leisure time and follow the directions on your paper.

1. In Switzerland we like to **go skiing** in the winter and **go hiking** in the summer.

2. In El Salvador we like to **play soccer** and **baseball** all year long.

3. In Germany we like to **listen to music** and **play** musical **instruments** —especially in the winter when we can't go outside.

4. In the United States we like to **play basketball** in the spring and **football** in the fall.

5. In England we **play tennis** in the spring and **go camping** in the summer.

6. In Japan we like to **go swimming** at the beach in the summer and **go to the movies** all year long.

7. In Greece we like to **go running** in the summer and, like a lot of people, we **watch TV** all year long.

■ What Holiday Is This?
Focused Listening II/Activity Sheet, p. 160

Listen to the people talk about holidays and follow the directions on your paper.

1. Roberto, go put on your cat costume. It's almost **6:30**. Time for trick or treating. You're going to be a very scary cat. (**Halloween**)

2. (Yawn) What time is it? **7:30** already? What is this? Flowers for me? Oh, I forgot it's **Valentine's Day**. Come here, sweet thing. Give me a kiss.

3. Okay, everyone. It's almost time. I'll make a toast! To a year of health and happiness and winning the lottery! 10 - 9 - 8 - 7 - 6 - 5 - 4 - 3 - 2 - 1 - **12:00**! **Happy New Year!**

4. We have a few more things to do, but let's decorate the tree later. The mailman is coming at **ten**. Let's sign the **Christmas** cards so we can give them to him.

5. **Nine o'clock**! They're starting. They're starting! Oooh! I love fireworks! I love the noise! I love the **4th of July**!.

6. Dan! Dan! The children will be here at **3:00** for the **Easter** egg hunt. Let's hide the eggs before they get here. I've saved some so that George and Barbara can paint them.

7. (Clock striking 7:00) **Seven o'clock**. Let's sit down, everyone. The food is all ready. Let's give thanks for all that we have and let's remember people that don't have as much as we do. (**Thanksgiving**)

8. Here, Chester. You take this flag and I'll take the small one. You can wave it when you see the soldiers. The **Memorial Day** parade starts at **2:00**. Let's hurry so that we can see everything.

■ **Match the sport to the country.**

a.

b.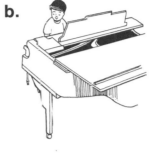

c.

d.

e.

f.

g.

1. __f__ Switzerland

2. _____ El Salvador

3. _____ Germany

4. _____ United States

5. _____ England

6. _____ Japan

7. _____ Greece

* tapescript on p. 158

Focused Listening II/Teacher's Notes, p. 3/Dictionary, pp. 94–95

■ **Fold your paper on the dotted line.**
■ **Listen and circle the correct holiday.**

1. Christmas	Valentine's Day	(Halloween)
2. Valentine's Day	Easter	Thanksgiving
3. Memorial Day	4th of July	New Year's
4. Christmas	Halloween	Valentine's Day
5. Easter	New Year's	4th of July
6. Thanksgiving	Memorial Day	Easter
7. 4th of July	Thanksgiving	Valentine's Day
8. Memorial Day	New Year's	Halloween

- - - - - - - - - - - - - - - - - - - FOLD HERE -

■ **Listen again and match the number to the correct time.**

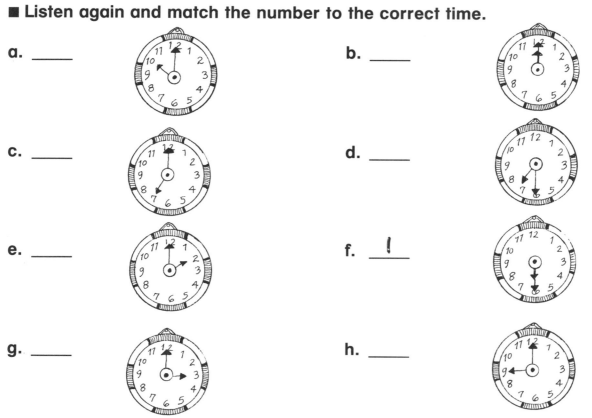

a. _____

b. _____

c. _____

d. _____

e. _____

f. __1__

g. _____

h. _____

* tapescript on p. 158

© 1994 Oxford University Press. Permission granted to reproduce for classroom use.

Happy New Year!

TPR Sequence/Teacher's Notes, p. 4/Dictionary, pp. 94–95

1.
Come to a New Year's Eve Party!
WHEN: Dec. 31 – 8:00 P.M.
WHERE: 5743 Adele Road
The Riddles

■ **Match the sentences to the pictures above.**

_____ Prepare the food.	_____ Clean up the house.
_____ Decorate the house.	_____ Kiss and hug.
1 Invite people to your party.	_____ Make a toast.
_____ Watch the clock.	_____ Relax.

1. ■ **Sit with a partner. Don't look at your partner's paper.**
   ■ **Look at the TV listings below.**
   ■ **Ask your partner questions, such as:**
       What's on Channel _____ at _____?
   ■ **Write the answers.**

TONIGHT ON TV

	7:00	7:30	8:00	8:30	9:00
2	News	Basketball			
3		All in the Family		Married with Children	That Girl
4	Football				
6					Music Around the World
8			Movie: Three Men and a Baby (PG13)		
9	Movie: Halloween 3 (R)				

2. ■ **Look at the TV listings.**
   ■ **Answer your partner's questions.**

1. ■ **Sit with a partner. Don't look at your partner's paper.**
   ■ **Look at the TV listings below.**
   ■ **Answer your partner's questions.**

TONIGHT ON TV

	7:00	7:30	8:00	8:30	9:00
2	News	Basketball			
3	I Love Lucy		My Three Sons	Married With Children	
4					
6	**Movie:** White Christmas				Music Around the World
8	Exercise with Emily				
9					

2. ■ **Look at the TV listings.**
   ■ **Ask your partner questions such as:**
       What's on Channel _____ at _____?
   ■ **Write the answers.**

Do You Play Basketball?

Mixer/Teacher's Notes, p. 6/Dictionary, pp. 92–93

■ **Walk around the room. Ask and answer this question:**

   Do you _____ *?*

■ **Write a different name in each space.**

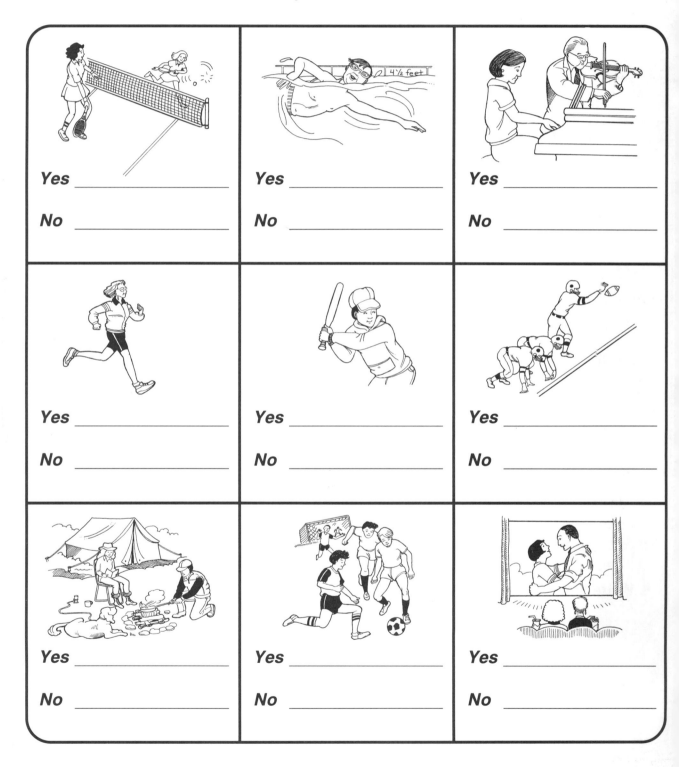

Yes _____	**Yes** _____	**Yes** _____
No _____	**No** _____	**No** _____
Yes _____	**Yes** _____	**Yes** _____
No _____	**No** _____	**No** _____
Yes _____	**Yes** _____	**Yes** _____
No _____	**No** _____	**No** _____

The Thanksgiving Tree

LEA Project/Teacher's Notes, p. 10/Dictionary, p. 95

THE PROJECT:

- **You are going to make a "Thanksgiving Tree."**
- **Your teacher will draw a tree like this:**

- **Then you will talk, write, and read about the experience.**

DIRECTIONS:

1. Talk about what you are thankful for with your classmates and teacher.

2. Get some <u>construction paper</u> and <u>scissors</u> from your teacher.

3. Cut out leaves and flowers. Be sure they are large so that you can write on them.

4. Draw one picture of something you are thankful for on each leaf or flower.

5. Tape your leaves and flowers on the tree. Tell your classmates about your picture.

6. Describe the tree to the teacher. (Your teacher will write what you say on the board.)

7. Look at the sentences on the board and copy them.

8. Read the sentences to a classmate.

Park Rules

■ **Read the park rules.**

■ **Circle these words:**

| camping | Christmas | hiking | picnic | swimming |

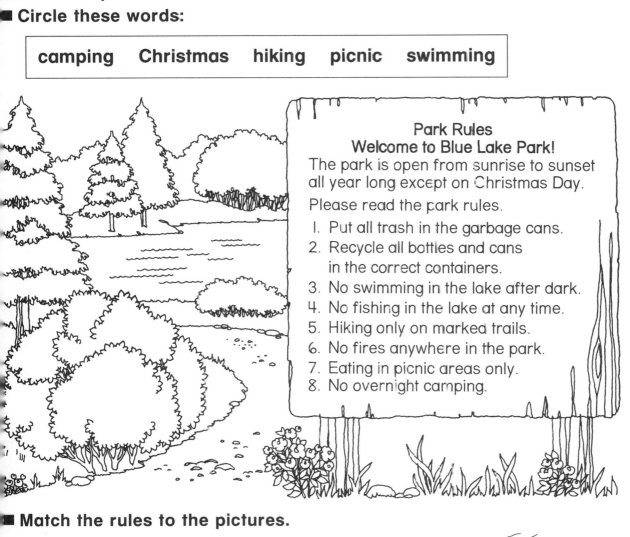

Park Rules
Welcome to Blue Lake Park!
The park is open from sunrise to sunset all year long except on Christmas Day.

Please read the park rules.

1. Put all trash in the garbage cans.
2. Recycle all bottles and cans in the correct containers.
3. No swimming in the lake after dark.
4. No fishing in the lake at any time.
5. Hiking only on marked trails.
6. No fires anywhere in the park.
7. Eating in picnic areas only.
8. No overnight camping.

■ **Match the rules to the pictures.**

a. _3_

b. _____

c. _____

d. _____

e. _____

f. _____

A Letter Home

Narrative Reading/Teacher's Notes, p. 12/Dictionary, pp. 94–95

~from the desk of Marta Morales~

Dear Tina,

How are you? This is my first letter in English. In class we are learning about American holidays. The Fourth of July is Independence Day. People watch fireworks in the park, have picnics, and play baseball. It is a lot of fun, but Thanksgiving is my favorite holiday. Everyone gets together with friends and family. Most people eat turkey.

Halloween is in October. My teacher says it's a holiday for children, but adults like to wear costumes too. Of course, many people here celebrate Easter and Christmas. They decorate pretty trees, just like at home. I like Christmas here, but I miss all of you.

That's all for now. You can see I'm learning a lot of English. Write soon!

　　　Love,
　　　　Marta

■ Draw a line to complete the sentence.

1. This letter is about　　　　　　　　　**a.** Marta.

2. This letter is from　　　　　　　　　　**b.** holidays.

3. This letter is to　　　　　　　　　　　**c.** Thanksgiving.

4. On Halloween adults wear　　　　　　**d.** Tina.

5. Many people watch fireworks on　　　**e.** costumes.

6. Marta's favorite holiday is　　　　　　**f.** The Fourth of July.

Appendix

Upper Case Letters

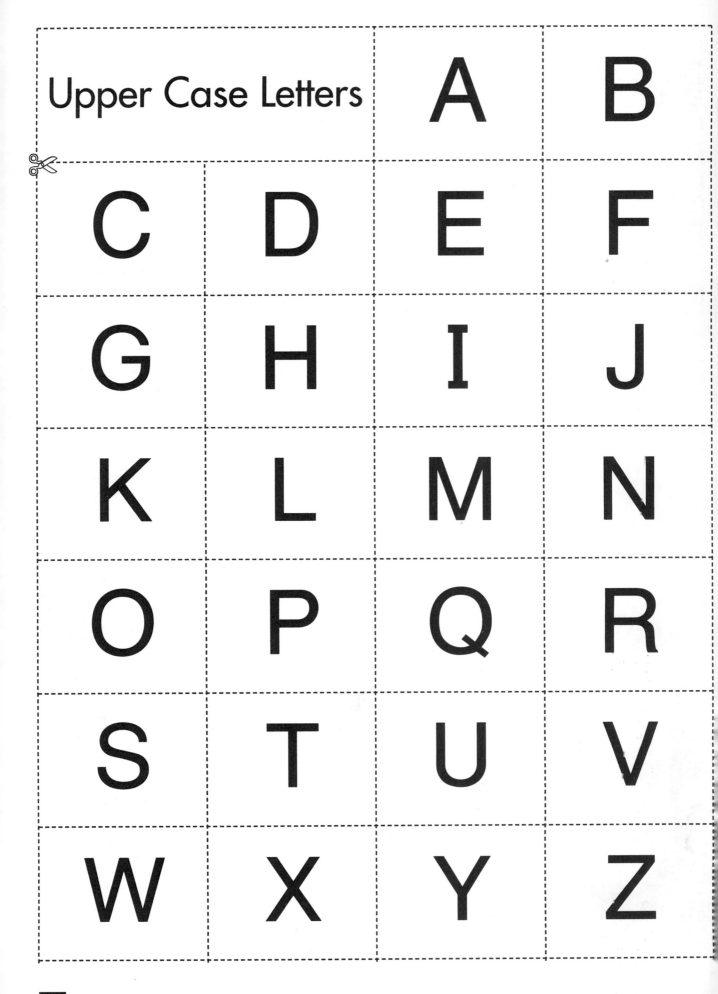

A B

C D E F

G H I J

K L M N

O P Q R

S T U V

W X Y Z

Lower Case Letters

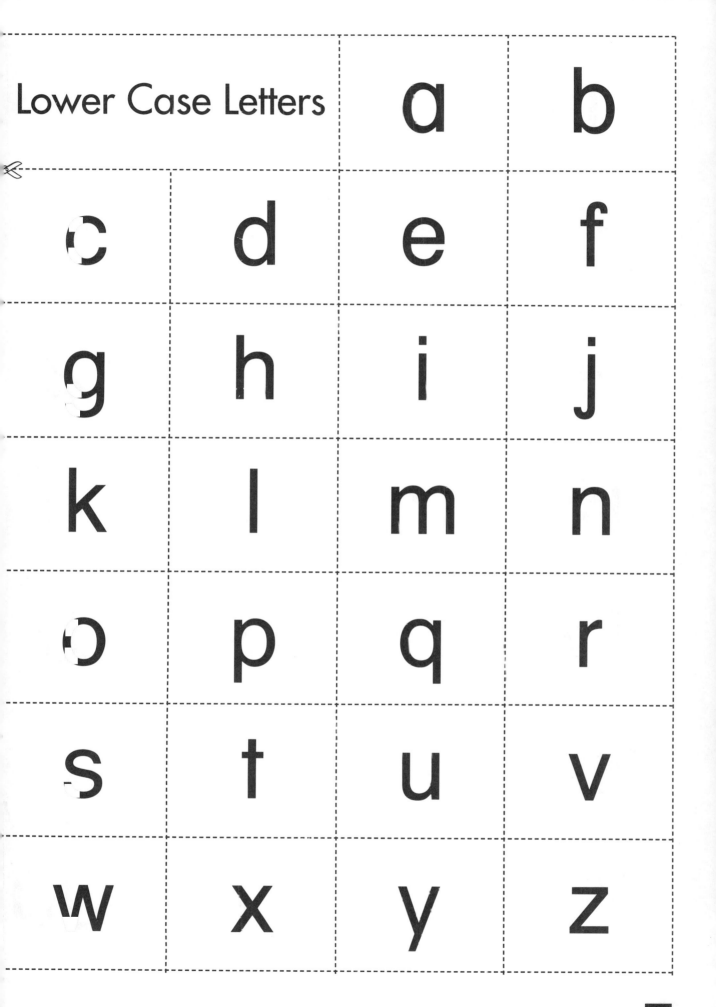

a b

c d e f

g h i j

k l m n

o p q r

s t u v

w x y z

1	2	3	4
5	6	7	8
9	10	11	12
13	14	15	16
17	18	19	20
30	40	50	60
70	80	90	100

Index

Acknowledgments

We would like to thank all the wonderful students, colleagues, and workshop participants who have inspired, supported, and encouraged us, far and wide, throughout the writing process.

We are also grateful to:

Margot Gramer for giving us her book to work with,

Helen Munch for her edits and advocacy,

Paul Phillips for his sense of aesthetics and humor,

Renée Weiss and Rheta Goldman for their help laying the groundwork,

Amy Schneider and Patty King for their thorough and excellent review,

Debra Shaw for her persistence and good sense,

Myra and Michael Baum for their technical support, and, of course, Susan Lanzano for providing us with cross-continental grouping strategies.

This book is dedicated to Pearl and Al for their creative urgings, to Mrs. Marvin for her tireless love and devotion, and to Ray and Dulcie Foster for a lifetime of encouragement.